THE NEW COUNTRY STYLE ENGLAND

THE NEW COUNTRY STYLE ENGLAND

PHOTOGRAPHS BY INGRID RASMUSSEN
TEXT BY CHLOE GRIMSHAW

WITH 580 COLOUR ILLUSTRATIONS

Thames & Hudson

Jacket and book design: Grade Design Consultants, London

First published in the United Kingdom in 2006 by
Thames & Hudson Ltd, 181A High Holborn,
London WC1V 7QX

www.thamesandhudson.com

© 2006 Thames & Hudson Ltd, London
Photographs © 2006 Ingrid Rasmussen
Text © 2006 Chloe Grimshaw

British Library Cataloguing-in-Publication Data
A catalogue record for this book is available from
the British Library

ISBN 13: 978-0-500-51290-6
ISBN 10: 0-500-51290-6

Printed in Singapore by CS Graphics

CONTENTS

INTRODUCTION 6

WALKING COUNTRY 14
Rustic Elegance 18
Cottage Baroque 28
Colonial Chic: The Victoria Hotel 38

FIELD AND STREAM 46
Global Traveller 50
Eclectic Interiors 58
Norfolk Minimalism 68
Grand Stately: The Ickworth Hotel 78

WOODLAND CLEARINGS 88
Gothic Modern 92
Rectory Reborn 102
Alhambra Abbey 112
Ranch Retreat 122
Weekend Luxury: Babington House 132

CLIFFS AND COASTLINES 142
Clifftop Georgian 146
Sculptor's Studio 152
Candlelit Cottage 160
Seaside Industrial 168
Island Escape 178
Nautical Haven: Hotel Tresanton 186

COUNTRY VILLAGE 196
Rural Retro 200
Theatrical Spectacle 208
Rich Tapestry 216
Cornish Grandeur: Fowey Hall 224

FARM 232
Rustic Reclaimed 236
Farmhouse Organic 244
Devon Pottery 254
Contemporary Country: Cowley Manor 262

DIRECTORY 270

INTRODUCTION

THE ENGLISH COUNTRYSIDE HAS LONG HAD A TIMELESS APPEAL, FROM RUSTIC PUBS TO CRICKET MATCHES ON THE VILLAGE GREEN, PICTURESQUE CHURCHES TO STONE-CLAD COTTAGES. WHETHER RAMBLING OVER ROLLING HILLS OR WALKING COASTAL PATHS, ENGLISH COUNTRY LIFE REPRESENTS AN ESCAPE FROM URBAN ILLS. THE COUNTRY LIFESTYLE HAS TRADITIONALLY BEEN ABOUT WELL-WORN COMFORT, FADING STATELY HOMES AND AFTERNOON TEA ON THE LAWN. BUT ALL THIS IS NOW CHANGING. A 'NEW COUNTRY STYLE' IS BEGINNING TO TAKE HOLD, IN COTTAGES, VILLAGES AND RURAL RETREATS ACROSS THE LAND.

This new style takes on many forms, but above all combines a creative, often modern sensibility with an unadulterated enjoyment of country pursuits. A new generation of city dwellers are seeking a more rural existence, not just as a contrast to their urban lifestyle, but as inspiration for their creative careers. Snapping up cottages, sprucing up inherited properties, reinterpreting vernacular buildings, these new country residents are injecting freshness and bright ideas into England's wonderfully idiosyncratic places and spaces.

Designers worldwide have taken inspiration from the English countryside, and what was once old and tired has been reinvented as 'shabby chic'. Traditional crafts have become fashionable again, and design-savvy homeowners are seeking out hand-made goods, from Clive Bowen's pots to Kaffe Fassett's textiles. It is all about having unusual and desirable pieces in your home, and discovering treasures at local markets and auctions. *The New Country Style England* reveals how traditional buildings have been adapted for contemporary use, from Victorian rectories and ancient barns to 1950s bungalows, to create unique modern homes.

Relocating to the countryside often means being able to afford a larger home and the chance to become part of a village community. The pressures of limited space and long working hours leave little time or money for creating an ideal home in the city, and exchanging a cramped urban flat for a sprawling farmhouse or rose-covered cottage can be a liberating experience. Petra Boase and Russell Hall left their London home for a two-up, two-down cottage in Norfolk with a pink front door. Despite the house's small proportions, the couple doubled their space by building a kitchen extension and garden shed outside, which now serves as Petra's office.

Owning a second home can seem like the ideal solution, but the weekly commute can be exhausting, especially with a young family. Richard and Arabella Parr used to divide their time between the city and the countryside, until Richard had enough and decided to move his architectural practice into one of the outbuildings surrounding their farmhouse. He is now much in demand as an architect and interior designer, converting neighbouring buildings into desirable contemporary homes.

Many families, such as the Stucleys and the Lawsons, have lived in the same house for generations, and have adapted their homes to suit their changing needs. Lord and Lady Stucley open up their twelfth-century abbey to the public for part of the week, and in the evenings this historic building becomes their own again. They have a relaxed approach to their home, and are happy for visitors to explore every part of the abbey. In Devon, it is a small mill cottage, rather than a grand and imposing house, that has been home to successive generations of Briony Lawson's family. A new gallery was added to the cottage in 2004, creating a light-filled corridor and exhibition space for Briony's sculptures. The extension has transformed the house, and Briony admits to spending most of her time there, enjoying the views of the Atlantic Ocean through the floor-to-ceiling windows.

The artist called Fish enjoys a nomadic lifestyle, roaming around the Gloucestershire countryside in his Romany gypsy wagon, warmed by a Victorian stove and lit by candles. Fish designs and builds his own caravans, makes shamanic drums, and holds workshops around the country at the summer festivals. A fellow artist, Clive Bowen, moved to Devon to work as a ceramicist forty years ago, and never left. He now lives at Shebbear Pottery, an old farmhouse that has now been converted into a family home, showroom and studio. Just as the ocean and surrounding woodland are daily sources of inspiration for Briony's organic sculptures and for Fish's crafts, so are the rich, earth tones of the Devon landscape inspiration for Clive's pottery. Even the clay that he uses comes from the local clay pit, just down the road.

Hotel owners have also been influenced by the new country style, recognizing that savvy guests are ever more appreciative of good design and individuality. They realize that sophisticated urban design does not always travel well to the country. 'There is no point in doing a chic London hotel in Cornwall,' hotelier Olga Polizzi explains. 'The colours of the sun and the sea are so strong that they ask to be repeated inside.' At Clovelly Court in Devon, the clifftop setting and the changing blues of the sea and sky dominate every room. The particular blue that is unique to Clovelly is featured in the house's French Wallpaper Room, overlooking the ocean.

Choosing furniture for a country house is a completely different prospect from fitting out an urban flat, and Agas and enormous farmers' tables tend not to fit in the latter's cramped spaces. For their Norfolk cottage, Petra and Russell looked for examples of British design, from vintage Hornsea pottery to traditional textiles, in the local charity shops, auctions and markets. Bringing the fruits of their searches home, the couple combined retro 1970s prints with 1950s chairs to create a riot of colour and texture. On the Sussex south coast, textile designers Brandon Mably and Kaffe Fassett also scoured the nearby shops to furnish their home, taking the area's soft light and mild climate as their inspiration. The resulting interior, incorporating patchwork curtains, needlepoint cushions, chinoiserie paintings and floral tapestries, bursts with colour. Such a strong design statement could be overwhelming, but the subtlety and sophistication of the décor creates a sensual home that is warm and inviting.

The redesign of an old stone farmhouse calls for freshness and simplicity. The late designer Peter Kent and editor Hamish Bowles created a modern backdrop to their house, keeping the flagstone floors and whitewashed walls and adding seagrass matting to the floors. All of the essential elements of country living are here, including oak-beamed ceilings, stone fireplaces and deep, freestanding baths. Their new home was designed to be a refuge from their hectic working lives, and to allow time for the gentler pursuits of the countryside, from tending the garden to catching up with friends around the kitchen table.

For architect Fiona Naylor and photographer Peter Marlow, the most appealing aspect of country living was to be cut off from modern technology, and consequently their home has no computer, television or telephone. They are free to explore the Dungeness beach and to live at the mercy of the elements. Inside their coastguard's tower, Fiona has also used a pared-down style for the design of their home. With one room on each floor, an industrial-steel staircase provides passage throughout the house. There are no interior doors, and even the smooth, stone flooring is kept simple.

This bold, contemporary approach to renovating ancient buildings can be very successful. Greville and Sophie Worthington knew that their neo-Gothic chapel in Yorkshire would form the perfect backdrop to their collection of modern Italian design, and, anxious to avoid the formal atmosphere often found in church conversions, the couple artfully arranged pieces from B&B Italia, Capellini and Pucci next to stained-glass windows and stone columns. A trampoline graces the upstairs chapel, and this formerly cold and draughty space now serves as the children's playroom.

Staying at country-house hotels has become an increasingly less spartan and more luxurious experience. Opening in 1998, Babington House was designed as the ultimate country retreat, and immediately had an enormous effect on English contemporary design. As if overnight, rambling country houses with lakes and croquet lawns went from being old-fashioned to incredibly chic. Inside, the atmosphere is one of decadent glamour, as if anything could happen within this atmospheric old house. The walls are painted in deep, rich colours, the sofas are comfortably battered, and the lighting, despite the ultra-modern fixtures, is soft. Following Babington's example of combining old and new, Luca Smit and Miles Leonard chose contemporary pieces for their Victorian rectory, including day beds from Lombok, sofas from The Conran Shop, rugs from Ikea and lighting from Liberty, and placed them next to the eighteenth- and nineteenth-century Dutch and Spanish furniture that Luca inherited from her father. With this modern approach, the heirloom pieces now make a bold and dramatic statement.

Modern farms present their own unique challenges. Finding the economic realities of farming too daunting, David Murray sold his farm and kept just fifty acres of land for his cattle, which allowed him the freedom to pursue his work as a furniture designer and to design his dream home. David has spent the past ten years converting an old cow byre on his land into an elegant farmhouse, built entirely from found materials and architectural salvage, including the flagstone floor of a derelict church. In Berkshire, concern for their natural surroundings led Peter and Juliet Kindersley to develop their 2,250 acres as an organic farm. Sheepdrove Farm is now a major research centre into environmentally sound farming methods.

Living in the countryside can be a new source of inspiration for your home. It is all about creating an individual look, taking the best from the past and updating it with modern sensibilities. Whether you are looking for peace and solitude or want to be part of village life, living in the countryside no longer means giving up creature comforts. New pleasures are to be found in the changing seasons, meandering down country lanes, and reading the papers in front of a roaring log fire. Gathered around the kitchen table with family and friends, followers of the new country style have time to relax and enjoy life.

WALKING COUNTRY

WALKING COUNTRY TAKES US OVER THE ROLLING HILLS OF THE COTSWOLDS
AND THROUGH ANCIENT NORFOLK WOODLAND. ENGLAND IS COVERED
BY A NETWORK OF BRIDLE-WAYS AND FOOTPATHS, WINDING THROUGH
UNSPOILT COUNTRYSIDE. TO DISCOVER THE BEST SPOTS, WE CLAMBER OVER
STILES, PUSH OPEN FIVE-BAR GATES AND WADE THROUGH STREAMS: THIS IS
WALKING COUNTRY AT ITS BEST. EACH OF THESE HOMES IS SURROUNDED
BY GRASSY MEADOWS, FIELDS AND FORESTS. INSPIRED BY THE LOCAL

LANDSCAPE, PETER KENT'S HOME IS A COOL, MODERN RETREAT WITH FURNITURE MADE FROM ENGLISH OAK AND SET AGAINST SIMPLE STONE FLOORING. TO CONTRAST WITH THE SOFT, GENTLE TONES OF THE MEADOW OUTSIDE THEIR FARMHOUSE WINDOW, THE PARRS CHOSE RICH, VIBRANT COLOURS FOR THE INTERIOR. THE VICTORIA HOTEL, SET IN THE HOLKHAM ESTATE IN NORFOLK, HAS A COMFORTABLE, WELL-WORN FEEL. ALL OF THESE COUNTRYSIDE DWELLINGS HAVE A PLACE FOR YOUR MUDDY WELLIES!

Rustic Elegance

THE LATE PETER KENT, DESIGNER and *bon viveur*, lived in an old farmhouse of Cotswolds stone in Gloucestershire, which he shared with Hamish Bowles, contributing editor at American *Vogue*. The previous tenant was Jasper Conran, and the couple inherited his cool, calm interior of white walls and simple seagrass matting.

Nestled in a Cotswold valley, the farmhouse is surrounded by fields of wheat, rolling hills and gentle woodland, with no other signs of habitation in sight. Internally, views are framed in doorways and windows, ensuring that the natural landscape is only ever a turn of the head away.

Despite creating some of the most elegant interior spaces in London, including fashion photographer Mario Testino's apartment, Peter felt that architecturally the farmhouse was 'such a fabulous space, it didn't need that much doing to it.' For Peter, living in the countryside was all about comfort, rather than perfectly designed interiors.

Peter and Hamish enjoyed entertaining friends and family, always striving to make their home as relaxed and welcoming as possible. Occasionally whole crowds would descend on the house for a summer picnic, with as many as twenty or thirty sitting outside in the garden. In the winter, Peter would build a roaring fire in the dining room and invite friends round for Sunday lunch. For large dinner parties, the couple would borrow an 1890s dining table, made from thick slabs of elm, from Hilles, the nearby Arts and Crafts manor house, built in 1913. The Aga was very much a part of Peter's enjoyment of

Arts and Crafts chairs from Alfie's Antique Market, in London, surround the dining table on a simple flagstone floor. The vase on the table and the paper lantern hanging above it are both from Habitat. On the window ledge is Cotswolds pottery from the 1940s and 1950s.

entertaining, and changed his approach to cooking. 'It is just so easy to cook with,' he said, 'and in the winter makes the kitchen warm and toasty. The Aga invites you to make something.'

Peter recalled that when visiting country houses as a child, what he found particularly cosy were all the books and 'funny paperbacks' in the different guest rooms. In his own house, he filled the bookshelves with books 'on every subject to appeal to everyone, from Agatha Christie to Albert Camus, to books about India and travel. I put by guests' beds the kind of books I think they would find fascinating.'

Peter loved the position of the farmhouse, enjoying especially not being able to see any of the neighbouring properties. Within the house's wonderful walled garden, the couple were able to realize their dream of having an English country garden, complete with foxgloves, daisies, thistles and hollyhocks. The walls' ability to retain heat allowed vines and fig trees to flourish.

Inside the house, Peter's favourite place was the top-floor bathroom, to escape to when the farmhouse was full of guests, and to lounge in the bath on the rare occasions when he had the house to himself. 'It is like a sanctuary or a really luxurious spa,' he explained, 'delicious and empty.' The room captures the evening sunlight and offers incredible views.

ARCHITECTURALLY EVERY SPACE IS VERY SIMPLE AND VERY

ENGLISH. BUT RATHER THAN A WARREN OF SMALL ROOMS,

THE INTERIOR CONTAINS ONLY A FEW BIG SPACES.

Beneath the oak rafters is the
elegant master bedroom. All of
the furniture had to be taken
apart before being passed up
the narrow staircase and
reassembled. Once put back
together, the brass bed was
painted with red oxide and
covered with a vintage quilt
from an American flea market.

Most of the furniture in the house was bought from the London auction houses in Lots Road and Christie's South Kensington, or from Tetbury, 'antiques central', the local town. Peter bought twelve antique chairs at auction for £150, which fit in perfectly with the age of the house. The dining table is surrounded by Arts and Crafts chairs from Alfie's Antique Market. A simple oak side table with a slate top was also purchased in London, and the 1970s Knoll lamp was found at a Paris flea market. Rustic-looking vases from Habitat (bought for £7 each) and Cotswolds pottery from the 1940s and 1950s complement each other on the windowsills. Round, white paper lanterns, also from Habitat, hang throughout the house.

The farmhouse's appeal for Peter lay in the simplicity – and Englishness – of the architecture. The interior is spacious, but is not divided into a warren of small rooms. There are three spare bedrooms, each with its own bathroom, to ensure that guests weren't faced with a queue during middle-of-the-night visits to the loo. A large hallway between the bedrooms functions as an upstairs sitting room, which before his death Peter had planned to turn into an office.

The sofa-bed in this room can be used to accommodate extra guests, and is covered in French linen and a Moroccan throw. Peter believed that Moroccan pieces, such as the leather-and-straw woven rug in the drawing room, can occasionally work in old English houses because of their 'slightly medieval' feel. There is also a bookshelf filled with 'brilliant flower books with amazing covers', which Peter and Hamish bought in the local villages.

Metal side tables, found in Tetbury and London, sit next to all of the beds and are

'WE HAVE A WONDERFUL WALLED GARDEN, A REAL ENGLISH COTTAGE GARDEN WITH FOXGLOVES, DAISIES, THISTLES AND HOLLYHOCKS. THE WALLS RETAIN HEAT AND ALLOW PLANTS TO FLOURISH.'

prized for their different patinas. The end bedroom contains a Gothic-style bookcase from a Paris flea market and a folding 'campaign' table, used by army officers in the eighteenth and nineteenth centuries for studying maps and battle plans during military campaigns. The multi-coloured antique quilt (see p. 24, right) on the bed is not something Peter would normally have chosen, but he admitted that he couldn't resist its charms after having seen the quilt hanging over the balustrade of a picture framer's shop in Westbourne Grove.

A narrow, wooden staircase leads to the master bedroom, an incredible loft room with a soaring pitched roof and original oak beams (see p. 24, left). The narrow staircase dictated what could be taken upstairs, and all pieces over a certain size had to be dismantled. On the bedside table is an extraordinary lamp, carved from tree branches, which was a gift to Peter on his fortieth birthday. 'An Italian in Tangiers gave it to me,' Peter remarked cheerfully, 'but then I had to bring it back on the plane!' The red-and-white striped rug on the floor is from the bustling seaside town of Essouira, in Morocco. By the bed is a chair bought from Christie's South Kensington, and described by Peter as one of the most unusual he had ever seen: 'It has a spoon-back in leather, but also incorporates wicker and

carved wood – a bit of everything.'

Despite the cool, white minimalist look of the house, Peter and Hamish created a warm and inviting home for friends to visit. The large kitchen and dining room allowed the couple to entertain on a scale that would be impossible in most London homes. Being in the countryside was also a means of escape, allowing time to tend the garden, cook over the Aga, and unwind from the stresses of urban life.

Among Peter's essential gardening tools were Hermès shears, used here to gather flowers from the garden in a trug from the local village fête. Peter lays the table for lunch: the table is from Spooner, a favourite shop in London, and the chairs are vintage pieces from Lillie Road, in Fulham.

Cottage Baroque

AN IDYLLIC COTSWOLDS VILLAGE surrounded
by gentle hills, lush forests and meadows
carpeted with buttercups, cowslips and daisies
is the setting for Yew Tree Farm, home of Richard
and Arabella Parr. Richard works as an architect
in a converted stable in the garden, while
Arabella looks after their three small children.

The couple met when they were both working in Madrid, and discovered a shared passion for Spanish style and design. Arabella used to import furniture from Spain, inspired by the rich, burnished colours of the local antiques and paintings, and examples of her finds can be seen throughout the house, providing a striking contrast to the more traditional English oak furniture.

Yew Tree Farm was built in the 1770s as a farmhouse, complete with hayloft, dairy and cowshed, and extended a hundred years later to its current size. Moving into the house in the mid-1990s, Richard's ambition was to breathe life back into the rather tired and sad-looking structure, beginning with painting the previously 'dead-salmon' drawing-room walls in a rich shade of forest green. Strong colours, rather than safe and subdued pastels,

are used throughout the house, with the intention that they will fade and mellow over the passing years.

Richard and Arabella compromised over the colour of the dining room (see p. 33), choosing a rich aubergine instead of the vibrant red favoured by Richard, or the deep intense crimson that Arabella wanted. This room is particularly successful at night, lit only by candlelight, when the focus shifts from the walls to friends, food and conversation.

Objects and artworks that have a special place in the couple's hearts fill the room, from the Spanish silver candlesticks on the dining table, to the eighteenth-century English furniture and twentieth-century drawings and engravings by British typographer and illustrator, Eric Gill. A French religious painting sits above the fireplace, on the far wall is a gilt

Charles V mirror, and an ornate lantern
made by the Spanish royal glassworks in the
eighteenth century hangs over the table.
Natural matting and cowhide rugs soften
the timber floor, and the table is covered with
antique linen and surrounded by four English
oak ladder-back chairs. This is a fabulous room
for entertaining, without being in the least
stiff and formal.

Upstairs, the master bedroom (see p. 35)
has scarlet lacquered floorboards, rich brown
velvet and linen curtains, and a red-and-brown
bedcover. These colours are reflected in the
burnished oak and walnut furniture placed
throughout the room, from the seventeenth-
century oak panel used as a headboard, to the
simple Spanish coffer acting as a window seat.
The English oak chest next to the bed dates
from the time of Charles II in the mid-

A picturesque eighteenth-
century farmhouse conceals
a dramatic interior inspired
by the Spanish Baroque.
Overleaf: The modern kitchen
has an olive-wood counter,
table, stools and flooring, and
is illuminated by state-of-the-
art Italian lighting. Whereas
the kitchen was designed to be
practical and functional, the
dining room is a more magical
space filled with prized
possessions.

'THE HOUSE WAS VERY MUCH DESIGNED TO

BE A FAMILY HOME, AND NOT AN EXAMPLE

OF MY WORK OR A STAGE SHOWPIECE.'

seventeenth century, and the watercolours were painted in the eighteenth century.

Walking through to the bathroom (see p. 34), you arrive in a thoroughly modern space with a wall of mirrors above a limestone sink, separated into three practical sections for washing and shaving. On the opposite wall is a deep bathtub and picture windows overlooking the garden. One small window frames a vivid green Lalique perfume bottle from the 1920s. To reflect the antique oak and walnut furniture in the bedroom, Richard chose a deep black walnut for the bathroom's walls, flooring and cupboards.

Intending to build a modern kitchen, Richard was nonetheless reluctant to touch the walls of Cotswolds stone. His solution was to build a floating screen of cupboards, which leave the top of the walls exposed. At the base of the cupboards, mirrored skirting heightens the 'floating' effect. Small windows above the stainless-steel worktops and the Aga frame jars and bottles to create miniature pictures. To unify the kitchen, the same piece of olive wood was used for the floor, table, chopping board and stools. The sink is set into an Italian limestone counter, and the entire kitchen can be spot-lit by the Italian lighting system.

The kitchen door leads straight out into the garden, which has an outdoor seating area carefully positioned to catch the sun throughout the day. The couple chose formal planting – trained lime trees and boxed hedges – at the entrance to the house, but the lawn is surrounded by informal, cottagey borders. At the end of the garden is a tree house, a duck pond and a chicken shed, which houses a hen for each of the children.

From the red lacquer floor and velvet bedcover to the burnished seventeenth-century chairs and oak chests, the bedroom is decorated in warm, rich tones. The choice of black walnut for the walls, floor and cupboards of the bathroom cleverly echoes the bedroom's opulent look. The round window was designed to perfectly frame the 1920s Lalique perfume bottle.

Such delightful country life seems idyllic, but the couple's son, Lando, admits to missing the London Underground!

Combining contemporary design with Spanish Baroque style and English antiques, Richard and Arabella have come up with a thoroughly modern take on the traditional English farmhouse. This is primarily a family home: a house to be lived in and enjoyed, and one that will fade and age with wear and look all the better for it.

THE BATHROOM USES RICH MATERIALS IN A CONTEMPORARY
WAY. IT IS A POETIC SPACE, WITH VIEWS ACROSS THE GARDENS
TO THE COUNTRYSIDE BEYOND.

COTTAGE BAROQUE

'OUR MOVE FROM LONDON TO THE COTSWOLDS WAS A HAPPY ACCIDENT. THE HOUSE IS CHEERFUL AND ROBUST, WITH NO PRETENSIONS, AND IS THE IDEAL ENVIRONMENT FOR THE CHILDREN.'

The walled garden is the perfect playground. The children are responsible for looking after the chickens and Lando is shown here holding a hen. Swinging in the white Mexican hammock (a birthday present from Arabella to Richard) are the two girls, Imo and Tati, with Buffy the dog keeping watch.

Colonial Chic

THE VICTORIA HOTEL, HOLKHAM, NORFOLK

THOMAS WILLIAM COKE OF NORFOLK bought the site for The Victoria Hotel in 1837, the same year that the eighteen-year-old Princess Victoria ascended the throne. Created Earl of Leicester by the new Queen, Coke showed his appreciation by naming the hotel in her honour. With building work completed in August 1838, The Victoria Hotel soon opened its doors to an admiring public.

This nineteenth-century inn is renowned for its delicious food, using fresh, local produce, and for its laid-back atmosphere. Locals are encouraged to pop in for a pint, and guests can relax on velvet sofas and chat with the owners, Tom and Polly Coke.

Viscount Coke and his wife, Polly, have overseen the most recent renovations to the inn, keeping the original doors from 1838 but completely redesigning the rest of the interior. Converting the rather run-down inn into a glamorous boutique hotel was a shared vision, and the revamped Victoria Hotel opened in 2002. Inspired by the Victoria's beautiful setting at the north entrance to Holkham Park, the couple realized that with a significant overhaul, the hotel could become 'a very magical bolt hole'. And it has the added benefit of being five minutes' walk from Holkham Beach, 'which is wonderful for children and nature lovers'.

The Victoria Hotel is a quirky mix of battered Victorian furniture and luxurious antique pieces from Rajasthan, in northwest India. With vibrant colours, textiles, paintings and rugs, the look and feel of the Victoria is essentially Colonial chic. Polly points out that several maharajahs in fact came to shooting parties at Holkham. She chose to work with a local interior designer, Miv Watts (mother of Hollywood actress Naomi), and to use the Raj as a continuing theme. Miv travelled to Rajasthan to buy nearly all of the furniture for the hotel, which arrived 'in a sealed container shortly before we opened!' Luckily the container held the complete set of tables and

chairs for the restaurant, as well as some of the antique wooden doors and beds.

When it came to designing the hotel's bedrooms, Tom and Polly wanted to create 'comfort and atmosphere', rather than cool, modern rooms. Each of the ten rooms is decorated individually, 'some with bright, bold colours to contrast with the Indian beds, and others paler and more tranquil to correspond with the seaside and coastal themes'.

The 'Raj' room is one of the most sought-after bedrooms, with its sea-green walls and four-poster teak bed covered with richly patterned textiles and a red brocade bolster. The bed is so high that sleepy guests require

TOM AND POLLY WERE INSPIRED BY THE HOTEL'S BEAUTIFUL SETTING, SITUATED AT THE ENTRANCE TO HOLKHAM PARK, AND OVERLOOKING A NATURE RESERVE NEXT TO HOLKHAM BEACH.

The lounge and living room on the ground floor are filled with a quirky mix of Victorian paintings and antiques, together with carved doors, screens and tables from the Rajasthan area in India.

a step to get into it; fortunately, a velvet footstool is tucked underneath the bed. Hanging from the ceiling is a green Moroccan glass lantern, while colourful Indian pictures and throws add more splashes of colour. A particularly striking portrait of a maharajah in a blue robe and turban hangs above the bed, while a rich, red Moroccan rug is draped at its foot. Leading into the bathroom, the flooring is slate and the walls a deep blue, creating a luxurious atmosphere for the large,

freestanding bath. This cobalt-blue room is a wonderful contrast to the warmer hues of the bedroom.

Other guest rooms are given names that reflect the surrounding landscape, including 'Stone', 'Marsh', 'Wash' and 'North Sea'. The simple, white 'Wash' bedroom was named after the Norfolk Wash, and has a rustic wooden bed, a cosy duvet and crisp, white bedding. A portrait of local hero Admiral Lord Nelson hangs over the bed, and a cream-

patterned Moroccan carpet provides the one decorative element. Polly explains that this room, with its grey slate bathroom, is 'a calmer, more tranquil bedroom, based on neutral, sandy colours and pebbles'.

Bedrooms have views across Holkham Park and the nature reserve, which comprises seven miles of windswept beaches, sand dunes and pine forests. On returning to the Victoria, walkers will find a special bar that welcomes dogs, complete with a terracotta floor to cope with muddy foot- and pawprints.

For a more glamorous experience, guests can relax in the lounge area with its vivid blue walls, Moroccan lanterns and vibrant wall hangings. There are velvet Rajasthan sofas to sink into and stacks of newspapers to read, and even a tapestry of an elephant that has been dressed in exotic robes. A wooden lattice-work sofa with red velvet seats, piled high with embroidered red-and-blue Indian cushions, is next to an ornate birdcage. On the low, wooden table is a bunch of bird-of-paradise flowers and a wooden bowl filled with lemons, oranges and limes. Continuing the Colonial theme, an enormous painting of a tiger in a gold frame hangs behind a small, black lacquer elephant and a Moroccan earthenware pot, called a *tagine*.

The small sitting room has a more formal, Victorian feel to it, with marble busts and paintings and ornaments in every corner (see p. 43). The room is painted dark green with white cornicing, and a Coke family portrait hangs above the marble fireplace. On either side of the mantelpiece are bookshelves lined with family treasures. Leather-bound books are placed next to a log basket and a glass case containing a stuffed heron, and two Moroccan leather pouffes lean against the fireplace. Books are piled up against a black marble bust in one corner, while a turquoise vase props up yet more books in another. A red velvet sofa with scrolled wooden arms stands behind a polished mahogany Indian table, itself sitting on a rich blue-and-red Persian rug.

The Victoria Hotel has brought a dose of boho-luxe and Indian warmth to the chilly north Norfolk coast, winning awards for both its luxurious bedrooms and delicious food. The fish and chips, wrapped in *The Daily Telegraph*, and the local oysters are worth a particular mention.

This green bedroom (opposite the Raj room) is an eclectic mix of Moroccan and Indian finds, including a treasured painting of a maharajah and a teak bed with printed-cotton throws. The red bolster and brocade armchair add a dash of English country-house chic.

THE COBALT-BLUE BATHROOM IS A WONDERFUL CONTRAST TO THE BOLDLY COLOURED 'RAJ' ROOM, WITH ITS VELVET SOFAS AND MOROCCAN THROWS.

FIELD AND STREAM

FROM THE WINDSWEPT MARSHES ON ENGLAND'S EAST COAST TO THE GENTLE MEADOWS AND RIVERS OF GLOUCESTERSHIRE, THESE LOCATIONS ARE ALL CLOSE TO THE ELEMENTS. SURROUNDED BY RIVERS, BROADS, CREEKS AND FENS, THE LANDSCAPE IS FILLED WITH BIRDS AND WILDLIFE, DRAWN TO THE REEDBEDS AND MARSHLAND. SITUATED IN A WATER MEADOW, MARSH VIEW IS AN UNCOMPROMISING MODERN BUILDING, AND MAKES A STRIKING LANDMARK IN THE NORFOLK LOWLANDS.

IN DEVON, THE SIEFF FAMILY HAVE TRAMPED A PATH IN THE FIELDS SURROUNDING THEIR FARMHOUSE DOWN TO THE RIVER. HIDDEN FROM VIEW AND SHADED BY COOL, GREEN BRANCHES, THE CRYSTAL-CLEAR WATER RUSHES OVER WELL-WORN STONES. LIVING IN A GYPSY CARAVAN IN A PRETTY COTSWOLDS VALLEY, THE ARTIST CALLED FISH DEPENDS ON THE SURROUNDING FIELDS AND STREAMS FOR BOTH INSPIRATION AND TO PROVIDE SHELTER AND SUSTENANCE AND THE TOOLS OF HIS TRADE.

Global Traveller

FISH IS AN ARTIST WHO LIVES and works
in a quiet valley in the Cotswolds. Making a
covered wagon his home, the woods supply
the raw materials for his work, and the nearby
river provides water for washing and drinking.
A small solar panel supplies Fish with all the
energy he needs. It is extremely important to
this enterprising craftsman to live in a way that
is environmentally friendly; when he eventually
moves on from this site, he is very proud that
there will be no trace of him left behind.

Fish is careful to use only reclaimed sources, or timber that he has collected himself from the woods and fields around his wagon. Using Dennis Harwood's *The English Gypsy Caravan* as a guide, he taught himself to build traditional Romany wagons by trial and error. 'The first one I made was pretty heavy,' Fish admits, 'because I used ash.' He now uses a combination of woods, including ash, elm and oak, to build lighter, more efficient wagons.

Despite his nomadic lifestyle, Fish is a welcoming host, and usually has a pot of coffee warming over a log fire, using an improvised grate made from horseshoes. Neighbours frequently drop by to sit round the campfire and chat with their host, and visitors arrive to view the progress on his latest wagon or shamanic drum. Fish is regularly invited to festivals around England, and when we meet him he is preparing to hold a series of drumming workshops at Glastonbury. 'I'm an artist,' he says, 'a traveller

and a hippy. I like all of those festivals. I still enjoy it, even though the season is really a summer of work.'

Fish makes 'running-horse' shamanic drums by steaming a section of green ash into a hoop, which is is then covered with deerskin. Horses or other animals are then painted onto the deerskin with henna and acrylic paint. The drum has a special role in shamanism, serving as the vehicle which carries the shaman into the other world.

To avoid the cold, dark winter months, Fish spends the season in India. Evidence of his travels can be seen inside the wagon, from the mirrored textiles to the shrine dedicated to the Indian goddess, Lakshmi. The bed is covered with a sarong over a hand-made peg-loom mattress. Weaving raw fleece around the loom as he speaks, Fish explains: 'It is a very basic loom. You lay out the strings on the ground, and then wind the wool around the pegs. That makes your weave.'

Backing onto woodland that leads down to a stream, this gypsy wagon sits in an idyllic Cotswolds valley. Living in peaceful harmony with his surroundings and keeping himself busy with his artistic endeavours is a life that suits Fish very well.

THE ROMANCE OF LIFE IN A GYPSY WAGON IS CAPTURED BY THE COLOURFUL DETAILS AND OVERALL FEELING OF COMFORT AND COSINESS.

As a craftsman, Fish has a sharp eye for colour and detail: textiles from India sit comfortably next to his own hand-made stained-glass window. Every detail has been carefully thought through to minimize environmental impact – candles and a wood-burning stove ensure that Fish does not waste electricity.

For warmth and heat within the wagon, Fish uses a small, Victorian cast-iron stove called a 'Queenie', a wood-burner that also takes coal and has two rings on top for cooking. 'It is very easy to light', he says. 'Once I'm in bed I let it go out and light it again in the morning.' A paraffin lamp next to the bed and brass candle-lamps light the interior. Just above the bed is a beautiful stained-glass window, which Fish made himself. Lying in bed and looking outside, smelling the wood smoke from the fire and enjoying the candlelight, all capture the romance of living in a wagon.

Fish explains the wagon-building process: 'I started with the axles from an old farm cart, and decided that I was going to build from the bottom up. The spokes are made from elm, and the rest of the wheel is made from ash and oak.' Each of the three woods is chosen specifically for its different function; elm, for example, is incredibly strong and does not split, and therefore is suitable for wheels.

The base of the wagon, known as 'the unders', is made from ash, a light yet sturdy wood that keeps the weight down while retaining the wagon's strength and structure. The front board is ash, but the rest of the body is pine, and to make it even lighter, Fish uses plywood: 'No MDF at all – ply-board is the nearest I come.' The wagon is covered with a rot-proof canvas with a layer of thick felt for insulation, and lined on the inside with velvet. A box at the rear of the wagon holds the basic necessities: cast-iron pots, a stainless-steel water jug, copper urn, kettle and coffee pot. It also prevents soot from covering his belongings. An area at the back is called the 'crouch', and is used as storage space for tools, a water bucket, a bale of hay for the horse, and a tethering pin.

Hanging underneath the wagon on a chain is an iron brake shoe, or 'drag' shoe. Essential

when going downhill, the drag shoe locks the wheel as the wagon slides down. 'People think going uphill is harder,' Fish says, 'but I find going downhill is a lot worse as you could get a runaway, which is a serious problem with all that weight.' Fish used to drive a two-wheel horse-drawn cart, but found that when driving down some of the larger hills in Wiltshire, he often had to jump out of the cart and stand behind it with a rope, acting as a human brake.

'I haven't travelled with this wagon,' he says, 'but I will take it out at some point. When I am driving, I don't sit on the wagon. Instead, I have long reins and drive from the side, close to the horse.' The current wagon is still in the process of being painted, and Fish has many more details to complete, including the front door, the wood panels and the scrollwork on the steps. The final step will be lining out the paintwork in gold. For a weatherproof finish, the wagon is coated with gloss paint and then topped with varnish intended for yachts.

Adjacent to the wagon, Fish has erected a yurt, built on an ash frame that concertinas up like a trellis into four sections. It has a willow roof, which was steamed into place, and in the winter Fish adds a thick felt cover, with canvas over the top. He cooks and sleeps in the wagon, and uses the yurt as a living space. The yurt also doubles as an exhibition gallery for Fish's drawings of wagons and local landscapes, his shamanic drums and his collection of singing bowls from northern India, which are made from seven different types of metal and resonate like bells.

Fish also turns his talents to making bow-top wagons for clients, and explains that 'for

around £6,000 you can have a permanent spare room, without the hassle of getting planning permission'. For anyone tempted to take their own wagon out for a spin, Fish finds the response travelling around Europe to be a bit friendlier than in England!

Metal tools and sturdy boots are essential tools for Fish's work as a carpenter. Details from around the campsite include paintings of deer and horses on deerskin and a tin kettle that burns on a grate made from horseshoes.

FISH NO LONGER DRIVES A TWO-WHEEL CART, FINDING THAT ON STEEPER HILLS HE OFTEN HAD TO RUN BEHIND THE CART WITH A ROPE, ACTING AS A HUMAN BRAKE.

Eclectic Interiors

LOOKING FOR A WEEKEND RETREAT in Devon, the Sieff family came across a rather monastic-looking house in a beautiful location, close to the sea and just a short walk from the River Yeo. Other buyers had been put off by the property, but as interior designers Diana and Simon could see its huge potential, particularly in the way the house was arranged around a central courtyard, 'just like a French house'. Diana used to holiday here as a child and fondly remembers the north Devon beaches, 'with that real westerly light, bright and vibrant'.

Simon and Diana take their boxer dogs Archie and Jago for long walks through the fields surrounding their house and down to the River Yeo, which borders the property. The master bedroom opens onto a small, wooden terrace, covered with pale-pink wild roses. Overleaf: Grouped in the windows are pieces by contemporary ceramicist John Spearman. In the sitting room, the cream sofa and lamp with its glass base were designed by the Sieffs themselves. Diana chose the portrait of a lady by an unknown artist for her 'quirky hat'.

Inspired by the herds of wild deer that populate the local Exmoor landscape, Simon and Diana commissioned an enormous chandelier, six feet across, made from antlers. It hangs above the dining-room table, which was also made to order from old floorboards. Dining chairs were snapped up from a tiny market in France. 'It is very unusual to get a whole set of chairs with arms', Diana explains. 'When you arrive at these big French fairs, there are rows and rows of lorries all going back to England, just waiting to take your furniture back for you.'

The signature Sieff style is apparent in the huge open-plan kitchen and dining room: a real mix of old and new, placing strong, dark antique furniture next to the light, modern kitchen. The bold lighting is from Habitat, and the wooden units were built by a local boat builder. The kitchen has a vast Belfast sink and

reconditioned Aga from the 1950s to perpetuate the feeling of a house that has been lived in for generations.

A large wooden cupboard is placed against the far wall of the kitchen-cum-dining-room, and appealed to Simon and Diana because of its very English looks, despite being found at an auction in northern France. It is unbelievably heavy and took twelve men to lift into place. Arranged along the top of the cupboard are what look like old pharmacy bottles, large and dark green. They are in fact ordinary bottles that Diana found and then decorated with tea-stained labels for that vintage look.

Dogs are very much part of family life, but not necessarily welcome in the kitchen. To keep their pets out, the family commissioned a wrought-iron gate from the local smithy, which still allows Archie and Jago to see the

action and not feel excluded. 'We don't want to lock them out,' Diana admits; 'in fact, we hardly ever close the gate!'

The 'flagstone' floors throughout the house are actually made from reconstituted concrete, set off by whitewashed walls. Against this striking contrast, Diana has placed an eighteenth-century bombe commode. Such a formal piece of furniture would ordinarily be made from mahogany in France; unusually, this particular commode came from a country workshop in Sweden, and is fashioned from ash and elm. In the drawing room is a rather feminine lampshade from Camden Market, which was originally above a billiard table. Diana enjoys imagining what that room must have originally looked like, 'with a pink silk lampshade in rather a butch environment'.

In the living room, chairs from the 1950s sit happily next to those from the eighteenth

'WE LIVED IN A BEAUTIFUL RURAL ENVIRONMENT IN OXFORDSHIRE, BUT I WANTED TO RETURN TO NORTH DEVON, WHERE I HAD SPENT HOLIDAYS AS A CHILD.'

century. Diana comments that her home is 'like every English person's house; a very eclectic mix of pieces that you have been left or given'. She readily admits that most of the furniture in the house is not that important, and that the décor is 'all about the mix'. Looking at one particular piece, Diana admits that it was inherited and that she would never have bought it herself.

In recent years, more and more people have sought out a contemporary look, and have shied away from antique furniture. 'You can go to Ikea and buy a fantastic sideboard for £200,' muses Diana; 'why would you want to spend £2,000 on an antique?' But she feels that she has done her 'modern thing', and is now ready to go back to antiques. As she acknowledges, it is not always easy to find the right balance.

Upstairs, the house was in far better condition than in the lower floor, and even had its original wooden floorboards. The only changes made to the rooms were cosmetic, such as painting white the orange tongue-and-groove pine walls in the bathroom, and adding a few old linen towels and a painting from a jumble sale.

In the spare bedroom, antique sheets hung over a plastic pole make simple curtains (see pp. 66–67). The headboard has been reupholstered with linen sheets, and the bed is covered with vintage linen and Ralph Lauren indigo cushions. Above the bed hangs an extraordinary painting, bought in the south of France, which portrays Flemish nuns looking out to sea, one of whom holds a prayer book in her hand. 'It is a very odd subject matter,' says Diana, 'and it is quite obvious that there's a huge storm brewing.'

63

'DEVON IS OUR SANCTUARY. THE NATURAL BEAUTY OF THE LANDSCAPE AND THE DESERTED SANDY BEACHES MAKE IT THE PERFECT PLACE FOR A PEACEFUL WEEKEND.'

Diana shells peas at the dining room table, which was made from old floorboards. This room formerly served as the cowshed, and would have had a cobbled floor. The set of elk antlers originally belonged to an animal from Norway or Sweden, and was bought from a local auction in north Devon.

Simon and Diana's innovative approach to design can be seen in the way they have used materials: the flagstone floor is made from reconstituted concrete, antique linen sheets have been used for curtains and to cover headboards, and the elegant tongue-and-groove panelling in the bathroom is fashioned from painted pine planks.

The master bedroom has tongue-and-groove flooring painted with Farrow and Ball colours, and is furnished with nineteenth-century pieces, including an English chest and a small French table. The balcony was rebuilt in 2003 after it fell apart, and Simon and Diana seized the opportunity to plant a particularly vigorous wild rose, chosen because 'it looks like a wild bramble rose that you would find by the river. We also loved its very blushing pink colour.'

This unique pairing of old and new combines simple design with elaborate custom-made pieces to create the quintessential English home.

'OUR TRADEMARK HAS ALWAYS BEEN MIXING UP OLD AND NEW PIECES. SIMON AND I CONTINUALLY TRAVEL TO AUCTIONS AROUND ENGLAND AND FRANCE TO FIND UNUSUAL ANTIQUES.'

Norfolk Minimalism

MARSH VIEW STARTED OUT as a 1950s bungalow before being given a new lease of life by owner Alison Mitchell and architect Patrick Lynch as a spectacular piece of modern design. The design of the house evolved in an organic fashion, when Alison and Patrick spent a day on Holkham beach searching for inspiration from the beautiful surroundings. Firmly believing that Patrick has captured the true spirit of the house and the area, Alison admits that she was probably his dream client. 'I think he was thrilled', she says, 'that I wanted something so odd and so different.'

As a fine-art weaver, Alison's work uses colour to play with distance and perspective, and to create illusions of space. Consequently, she was able to see the potential behind this unpromising bungalow, which faced away from the striking view of a windmill and water mill beyond. Tall willow trees in the garden rustle in the easterly breeze, and just beyond them is a water meadow that leads down to the salt marshes, which, in turn, reach out to the sea.

Initially, Alison was keen to save money by simply building the living room and breakfast room, and leaving the rest of the bungalow as it was. She eventually realized that this would result in a one-bedroom house 'with one massive space', which she admits would have looked odd and not been the design statement she wanted. After consulting Patrick, Alison decided to put everything she had into the house, a difficult and potentially risky decision. 'But at the end of the day,' she says, 'I have got a lovely house.'

Phase two of the design process involved planning a kitchen and dining area, a second living room-cum-study, a bedroom and a bathroom, and two more bedrooms tucked under the pitched roof. The exterior of the house is made from black-painted bricks and timber, inspired in part by the angular shape of the local Norfolk windmills. Patrick suggested cladding the interior of the house in birch plywood to give the house warmth and structure. Light pours into the house, reaching the bedrooms, staircase and breakfast room first thing in the morning, and by lunchtime light is streaming into the living room.

Alison's daily routine is to track the sun as it moves around the house, starting in the breakfast room, where she comes to 'have a cup of coffee and look out at the view'. She also checks on the six owls and the marsh

'FROM AN ARCHITECT'S POINT OF VIEW, PATRICK WAS OVERJOYED THAT I WANTED SOMETHING SO BOLD AND SO UNUSUAL.'

harrier who make a habit of flying past the window at breakfast time. Whiling away the afternoons in the living room, she has noticed several red-legged partridges that parade in front of the glass and look at themselves curiously in the reflection. 'They are amazing', she says, 'and very funny.' Friends gather round the kitchen table, perched on Robin Day chairs, while in the breakfast room they sit on minimalist stools from Unto This Last, in London. Alison is at pains to point out that although she appreciates good design, such as the laser-cut plywood designs from Unto This Last, most of the objects and furniture has either been given to her or has been picked up cheaply.

Part of the architect's brief was to open up the vistas around the house by designing windows with no heavy uprights or divides. In the breakfast room, the window runs along the room's length and continues around the corner to permit views of an L-shaped slice of the garden. The room has real character, with a 'kissing bench' from Alison's aunt along one

The design of the house reflects the bare and dramatic landscape of the north Norfolk coast, and echoes the black windmill and the old mill buildings of the local seaside towns.

This corner window in the breakfast room captures the early morning light. Vintage leather armchairs are arranged around the fireplace in the living room, which overlooks the garden and the marshes beyond.

wall, and a stylish round rug on the floor from her mother's house, which she has always coveted.

Since she visited as a child, Alison has been drawn to the isolated and windswept north Norfolk coast. 'I love the fact that the telegraph wires end here', she says. 'It feels very much like you are on the edge of things.' The house, with its weather-worn, battered shape, echoes the natural landscape of wind-flattened marsh grasses. 'It is such a fantastic space, so beautiful

and so elemental', Alison explains. 'The house reflects back at you where you are in life, because it is such an uncompromising space.'

With the dramatic shape of the house and the constantly changing landscape, it is not surprising that Alison decided to keep the interior design as simple as possible. Walls are clad in birch plywood, and the floor is made from poured black concrete. Alison explained to Patrick that in the living room she wanted a high chimney with a skylight

at the top, and happily the resulting design was exactly what she had in mind. Vintage leather chairs and a low, wooden coffee table, made by a friend, are arranged around the fire. A simple Muji sofabed is at the opposite end of the room to accommodate spillover guests. It is next to a schoolhouse table, which 'has never looked as beautiful as it does here', Alison says. 'I love that table.' Ornamentation is kept to a minimum, with just two sculptural wooden bowls from Ikea and Unto This Last placed next to vases, and a solitary antler on the window ledge.

The two upstairs bedrooms are warm and cosy. The smaller one is intended for friends' children, with twin beds, bright bedspreads of crocheted squares, and a bird-patterned rug. The other bedroom has a large bed, a wooden chair from Alison's aunt, and a stunning view out over the marsh.

The original one-bedroom bungalow is now almost unrecognizable. Alison and Patrick have redefined the concept of a country cottage, bringing light and space into a previously small, cramped building. The house can now comfortably accommodate family and guests, without a chintz sofa or an Aga in sight.

'THIS HOUSE IS A VERY UNCOMPROMISING SPACE, AND MIGHT FEEL UNCOMFORTABLE IF YOU NEED A LOT OF CHINTZ AROUND YOU, AS SOME PEOPLE DO.'

Local reeds and grasses are displayed against the birch plywood walls. Raffia footstools and fruit bowls made from straw continue this natural theme. The plywood stools in the breakfast room, arranged along the work bench, are made by Unto This Last, in London's Brick Lane.

Light streams down the staircase, giving warmth and depth to the birch plywood surfaces. On the top floor, two guest bedrooms are tucked beneath skylights. Treasured books, cosy crocheted rugs and hand-painted furniture make these rooms feel warm and inviting.

THIS FORMERLY NONDESCRIPT BUNGALOW HAS BEEN TRANSFORMED INTO A BEAUTIFUL PIECE OF MODERN DESIGN: LIGHT, SPACIOUS AND WELCOMING.

Grand Stately

THE ICKWORTH HOTEL, BURY ST EDMUNDS, SUFFOLK

STAYING AT THE ICKWORTH HOTEL is all about exploring the grounds: over 1,800 acres of ancient deer parkland, walled gardens, lakes, vineyards and woodland. Most of the park was designed and laid out by 'Capability' Brown in the eighteenth century, and is considered to be one of England's most beautiful estates. Guests can discover the park on foot, or cover more ground by borrowing a bicycle and setting off on one of the cycle trails or booking riding lessons at the restored eighteenth-century stables.

The Ickworth is very much a family hotel. When we arrive for breakfast, there are several babies in the conservatory and all kinds of child-friendly menus available. Only ten years ago, however, the house had a much racier reputation when it was home to the Hervey family, who lived at Ickworth for almost two hundred years. Among a roster of notorious predecessors, Victor, 6th Marquess of Bristol was particularly notable for being sent to prison in the 1930s for his part in a jewellery heist at a Mayfair hotel. When he died in 1985 living as a tax exile in Monaco, the house passed to his eldest son, John, who died tragically early at the age of 44.

With the house and grounds now belonging to the National Trust, in 1997 the decision was made to turn the east wing of the house into a luxury hotel. Of the over 180 bids from different companies, the National Trust eventually chose Luxury Family Hotels, a company known for its gentle approach to conversion, to take on the project. The entire renovation scheme was completed in just nine months, at a total cost of £4.5 million.

The company's chairman, Nigel Chapman, knew that the conversion could not 'mimic what had been there before', and decided to approach the project in a contemporary fashion, rather than going down the traditional country-house route of velvet curtains, chintzy sofas and cumbersome furniture. He felt confident that he could blend old and new together, combining antiques with modern lighting and works of art. The company believed that future guests would be keen to relive the country-house experience, but with one key difference.

'Grand country hotels used to impose strict dress codes and have inflexible meal times', Nigel says. 'But now guests want a more freestyle experience, and not the same degree of structure.'

Luxury Family Hotels have undertaken much of the interior design themselves, and purchase antiques from dealers and importers, rather than from the more expensive antiques shops. The décor includes some modern furniture, but Nigel tends to opt for classic Italian design, including pieces from B&B Italia. Ickworth's new, sophisticated look was aimed at the current breed of well-informed hotel guests, who have become ever more knowledgable about contemporary design.

The modern theme is continued in the drawing room, with its 1960s designs by Eero Saarinen, including the white 'Tulip' chairs and stools. The sweeping staircase in the hallway has a more traditional feel, with an antique sofa on the landing covered in striped fabric from Osborne & Little. The lighting throughout was designed by Kevin McCloud, presenter of the popular television programme, *Grand Designs*.

In the library, bold cushions by Jonathan Adler liven up curved, 1950s armchairs by Marco Zanuso, which stand next to a Florence Knoll glass-and-chrome table. Vintage leather sofas and an antique lampshade sit alongside leather chairs from the 1950s, also designed by Florence Knoll. A portrait of Francesca, Marchioness of Bristol (b. 1965) by artist Matthew Carr hangs on the far wall.

One of the first-floor bedrooms also demonstrates this mix of nineteenth- and

Making the most of the great outdoors at Ickworth: guests can borrow bicycles or book horses to explore the grounds, designed by 'Capability' Brown in the eighteenth century. The house has a central rotunda, inspired by the 4th Earl of Bristol's experiences in Italy on the Grand Tour, flanked by two wings.
Previous page: Detail of the nineteenth-century entrance hall, made of inlaid marble.

twentieth-century pieces. A contemporary painting by Gillian McCormick hangs above an Italian Renaissance-style bed, made from burnished walnut, which dates to 1880 (see p. 86). Also made of walnut is the 1920s Spanish sofa, designed for afternoon siestas.

Nigel commissioned three artists to create new work for the Ickworth Hotel. Having learned from past experience, he explains that 'you have to let the artists get on with it, and become absorbed in the whole story of

Ickworth. They will feel it; you cannot tell them how to interpret it.' The work of Spanish artist Suzy Gomez, 'with its statuesque dimensions and heroic figures', dominates the entrance hall and main drawing room, whereas Judy Willoughby's paintings, inspired by her stays at the hotel, hang in the top gallery. The third artist, Bobby Pilsnier, was commissioned to create paintings which would 'capture something of the spirit of the place' for the dining room.

Original wooden doors and mouldings in the library contrast with cushions by Jonathan Adler, 1950s chairs by Marco Zanuso and a glass-and-chrome table by Florence Knoll. The portrait is of Francesca Hervey, the last marchioness to live at Ickworth.

The drawing room has vintage 1960s designs by Eero Saarinen, including 'Tulip' chairs and stools supplied by cult store Twentytwentyone. Tucked into an alcove on the main staircase, an antique sofa has been covered with striped fabric from Osborne & Little .

In the eighteenth century, wealthy tourists, including Frederick Hervey, 4th Earl of Bristol (1730-1803), flocked to Europe for the Grand Tour and to see the sights. So inspired was Hervey by his tour of Italy, that upon his return he built the suitably grand and Italianate Ickworth Hall, with its central rotunda and two wings on either side. The rotunda still houses his magnificent collection of Old Masters, including works by Titian and Velázquez, and portraits by Gainsborough and Reynolds, along with exquisite furniture, silver and porcelain.

Today, modern English tourists, tiring of the delays and discomforts of travelling abroad, find that very often they prefer a holiday in their native countryside. With so many country hotels offering every comfort, beleaguered urban guests are now spoilt for choice. The Ickworth Hotel offers the restorative benefits of the countryside together with modern sophistication and all the comforts of a luxury hotel.

84

'THE DRAWING ROOM WAS DESIGNED AS A CONTEMPORARY
SALON, A PLACE IN WHICH TO MEET FRIENDS AND RELAX.
ALL OF THE FURNITURE WAS DESIGNED TO IMPROVE WITH
AGE, FROM THE ANTIQUE PIECES TO THE LEATHER ARMCHAIRS.'

Antique furniture in the bedroom contrasts with the contemporary bedcoverings and artwork. The decorative table lamp, made from amber-coloured glass and dating to 1940, is placed in front of a Rococo gilt mirror, both from L&P Antiques, in Walsall. The Italian Renaissance-style bed is made from walnut, as is the Spanish day bed in front of it.

WOODLAND CLEARINGS

WHEN WALKING THROUGH WOODLAND, ONE OFTEN CATCHES A GLIMPSE
OF THE HIDDEN RUIN OF AN ABBEY OR A CHURCH TUCKED AWAY FROM
THE REST OF THE WORLD. SUCH ECCLESIASTICAL BUILDINGS — FROM
A NEO-GOTHIC CHAPEL IN YORKSHIRE, TO A VICTORIAN RECTORY IN
GLOUCESTERSHIRE, TO THE TWELFTH-CENTURY HARTLAND ABBEY IN DEVON
— ARE NOW MUCH SOUGHT-AFTER HOMES. MORE SECULAR HOUSES AND
HOTELS REWORK THEIR SYLVAN SETTINGS WITH A MODERN TWIST. AT CLIFF

BARNS IN NORFOLK, DESIGNERS RUSSELL HALL AND SHAUN CLARKSON
HAVE DRAWN INSPIRATION FROM THEIR SURROUNDINGS AND USED SILVER
BIRCH AND ROUGHLY-CHOPPED LOGS TO CREATE DRAMATIC DECORATIVE
FLOURISHES. AND AT BABINGTON HOUSE IN GLOUCESTERSHIRE, DESIGNER
ILSE CRAWFORD CREATED HER OWN WITTILY IRONIC TAKE ON TRADITIONAL
COUNTRY-HOUSE WOOD PANELLING BY CREATING ONE WALL OUT OF
STACKED LOGS, AND PAPERING ANOTHER WITH A WOOD PRINT.

Gothic Modern

TWENTY YEARS AGO, GREVILLE Worthington purchased an abandoned Catholic church in a remote part of north Yorkshire. Built between 1823 and 1832, the church seems to have been a 'coming-out-of-the-closet for Catholics in a way', says Greville, reflected in the 'tremendous neo-Gothic celebration' of its architecture. When Greville acquired the chapel in the 1980s, it had fallen into disrepair, but with the help of English Heritage he has been able to restore the chapel to something resembling its former glory.

Greville is a local Yorkshireman who runs the Catterick Sunday Market and admits to having a 'terrible need to collect'. He has become obsessed with bamboo, and has the largest single collection of it in England. He also makes and sells furniture, and is a trustee for a number of art foundations, including the Yorkshire Sculpture Park. In addition to all of these artistic pursuits, Greville is now starting to build up a collection of contemporary art.

Before you even step through the front door, Greville's passion for bamboo is evident. 'I grow every single species of bamboo that can survive in this climate', he says. 'It has been the most rewarding hobby because they are all doing pretty well.' His treasured plants are clustered at three sites: a sheltered location in the woods, an ornamental lake, and just in front of the chapel, where only the very hardy ones survive because of the 'terrible winds that lash in from Siberia'.

Shelter from the fierce north Yorkshire climate is found in the small, walled garden, entered through a wooden door sporting a lattice screen that is carved to look like bamboo. 'I made the doors to give the garden an intimate feel', explains Greville. 'The best way to be outside is in a small, enclosed area.'

Evidence of his wife Sophie's passion for collecting can be seen inside the chapel. In the living room, beautiful Capellini chairs are upholstered in Pucci prints, and complemented by the seductive 'Flap' sofa in soft, white leather by Italian design store Edra. For warmth, the family commissioned a wood-burning stove from the local ironmonger, which they cosy up to on pink chairs from Mint, in London, and a B&B Italia sofa piled

Deep in the heart of Yorkshire, a neglected stone chapel has been brought back to life. Gravestones and various carvings and statuary remain, but this is now a family home, framed by woodland and swathes of wild bamboo.

'THIS PLACE WAS ABANDONED AND PRETTY HORRIBLE, AND I HAD RUN OUT OF MONEY. THEN I GOT MARRIED, PULLED MYSELF TOGETHER, AND HERE WE ARE.'

CONTRASTING WITH THE STONE WALLS OF THE CHAPEL ARE
SENSUAL PIECES OF MODERN FURNITURE, SUCH AS THE
SINUOUS LEATHER SOFA AND THE PUCCI-COVERED CHAIR.

high with cushions. The furniture works well with Greville's collection of contemporary art by Langlands & Bell, Richard Long, Craigie Aitchison, Donald Judd and Catherine Yass.

Looking like it, too, could be a piece of contemporary sculpture is the Roman bath, which the couple found out in the garden. Greville's one family heirloom from his ancestral home, Brough Hall, is the dining table, which was carved from a single piece of oak to commemorate the end of World War II. Surrounded by Arne Jacobsen chairs, the table displays a line of simple, white pots by Edmund de Wall.

The focus of the warm and intimate master bedroom is the bed, covered with a chocolate-brown satin quilt from London's Space Boudoir and pink cushions and pillows (see p. 98). Greville bought the Chinese chest from a local auction, along with the huge Andreas Gursky photograph hanging above the bed, and built a shelf for Sophie's clothes from a curved piece of wood. An array of bright prints and colours occupies the space below, in which stands an elegant pair of silver-sequinned Marni shoes.

The bathroom has a sculptural wooden bath designed by John Pawson, and a Jenny Holzer sign, bearing the motto 'Cleanliness is

The ground floor of the chapel is now a glamorous dining room, filled with contemporary art and sleek Italian furniture that contrast with the dark, granite walls. It makes the perfect entertaining space for Greville and Sophie's eclectic group of friends; local neighbours rub shoulders with the cream of British artists.

next...', is propped up in the fireplace, showing a relaxed approach to godliness in this chapel. Rows of kaftans from trips to Morocco hang on wooden pegs above a pile of leather slippers and cosy sheepskins.

In the children's bedroom, thirteen Damien Hirst prints hang above twin Ikea beds, and Donald Judd drawings decorate the spare bedroom. 'Somehow it is all you need by Judd', Greville explains. 'A sort of memory of colour is enough.'

Greville and Sophie have realized their ambition to create a family home from an abandoned chapel in Yorkshire by combining the best of international contemporary furniture with a unique and personal collection of contemporary art. But perhaps Greville's most fulfilling achievement was to persuade Sophie, a dedicated West London girl, to share his dream.

USING A PALETTE OF SOFT PINK AND CHOCOLATE-
BROWN, SOPHIE HAS CREATED A SENSUOUS
ATMOSPHERE IN THE BEDROOM.

Wall-mounted lamps in the bedroom can be angled to provide suitable lighting for the books and magazines stacked nearby. In the bathroom, the family is kept squeaky clean with regular dips in the characteristically minimalist John Pawson tub, designed for Capellini. Overleaf: Light streams in through the stained-glass chapel windows, illuminating the children's trampoline, perfect for this double-height space.

Rectory Reborn

IT IS HARD TO IMAGINE MILES Leonard, managing director of Parlophone who works with such artists as Kylie and Coldplay, slowing down and relaxing in the countryside. Encouraged by his wife Luca, a freelance television director, the couple decided to find a place in the country in which to unwind from the demands of the city. Coming across a Victorian neo-Gothic rectory for sale in Gloucestershire seemed like the perfect start to the new year in 2004, and to a new life.

Months later, with the completion date ever more delayed, Miles and Luca began to measure rooms and look for furniture, buying basics for the house in the January sales. 'It is a mistake to rush things', Luca explains. 'You need to get a feel for what extra bits to add. We are quite lucky that we are equally interested in design, and have the same sort of taste and ideas about things.'

Every weekend is now spent in the countryside, but not in rural isolation. Friends and family often come to stay, and more and more weekends are spent entertaining rather than spending them on their own. 'There are impromptu visits as well', Luca adds. 'We like the idea of our house being somewhere people can just drop in.'

Rustling up breakfast for twelve guests, or hosting an unscheduled lunch, is no problem for the culinarily-inclined Luca. Just down the road is a fantastic farm shop where the couple stock up for those last-minute weekend visits. Unsurprisingly, the kitchen is Luca's favourite part of the house. 'It is a great room,' she says; 'a summer room, a winter room, an everything room.' With the Aga gently heating the kitchen and a large table for hungry diners, it is the perfect breakfast room on a Sunday morning. Hand-blown Italian glass lighting is from Liberty and was spotted by Miles who immediately fell in love with it. 'The rest of the house is quite traditional,' he says, 'and so we like little accents of more modern pieces.'

Stunning views of the countryside led Miles and Luca to choose the corner room at the top of the house as their bedroom, noting that 'it has the best view of the garden, and you can see the Mendip Hills leading to the Cheddar Gorge and Glastonbury Tor'. More immediate views look out onto the tower at the corner of the house and the branches of the ancient cedar tree in the garden. 'It is so peaceful waking up in the morning', says Luca. 'The first thing we do is pull back the curtains to see this incredible view.'

Wanting a clean and fresh feel to their bedroom, Miles and Luca contrasted dark wooden furniture from Lombok with cream linen curtains and white bedding. The furniture is particularly successful, notes Miles, because of its 'well-worn, old feel'. Cast-iron window frames are the only drawback to this airy room, as they tend to expand in hot weather and shrink in the cold, snapping the panes of glass. Occasionally the couple will hear 'a pop and a ping' as the glass moves.

Miles and Luca wanted to make each room different, and give each one its own character. The 'Shaker' room downstairs has a slightly modern feel to it, with its blue walls and teak four-poster bed, also from Lombok, made up with crisp, white sheets (see p. 111). Even older than the house is the huge cedar tree that can be seen from this room. At 350 years old, the tree has been nicknamed 'the wise old man' and can be seen for miles around.

Next door to the village church, in the heart of the Cotswolds, this Gothic rectory was just what Miles and Luca were looking for. The formal façade is deceiving; inside, the home is relaxed, and friends are encouraged to drop round at any time.
Previous page: The Gothic-inspired metal-and-glass staircase rises from the double-height hallway to the first floor.

'A NEW HOUSE NEEDS TO BE LIVED IN BEFORE YOU CAN DECIDE WHAT TO ADD OR HOW TO STYLE IT.'

To reflect the house's origins as a neo-Gothic rectory, Luca placed a small icon and a candle in the hallway. Many of the Spanish and Dutch antiques in the house were inherited from Luca's father, including the chair beneath the windows in the hall.

Another guest bedroom is what Luca terms their 'cottagey sort of room', because of its cast-iron bed from an architectural salvage yard in Sussex. There were hundreds of beds to choose from, but Luca was looking for 'a rounded shape, rather than one that was straight across, like a gate'. From the start, the couple had this room in mind for the Sussex bed, 'because it is a sweet little room'. 'We wanted something that was quite delicate,' Miles explains, 'rather than a shiny brass bed,

which would have looked a bit garish.'

On the first-floor landing is a tall, hollow sculpture made from the trunk of a palm tree from Indonesia. Its ridges have been smoothed off, and it was then sanded down and polished to create a favourite – if rather unusual – work of art (see p. 110). Hanging from the ceiling above the staircase is a vintage crystal-and-metal chandelier from Liberty, in London (see p. 103). Trawling round Liberty for such decorative touches was 'a real eye-opener', says

Miles, 'because we found so many things.'

The three arches that now make up the hallway formerly surrounded the original portico, where carriages would draw up to deposit their passengers. Guests would then be shown through to the reception room to warm up by the fire. Now the sitting room, this room still has its original fireplace. Luca imagined having loads of friends around 'a huge roaring fire on a winter's night', and began searching for the perfect sofa. The

couple eventually found just the one from The Conran Shop; large enough to fit the scale of the fireplace, but also 'slouchy and informal, nothing too structured'. Because the sitting room is quite dark, with a long window at the end, it was important to Luca to create a 'relaxed area where you can chill out and put your feet up'.

When Luca's father died in 2001, the family house was sold and the furniture and paintings were put into storage. Half-Dutch

Luca inherited the Victorian table and chairs, and has placed them next to a contemporary day bed, covered with an Ikea throw and silk cushions. Collected from her travels, the Moroccan and Turkish textiles have been made into large floor cushions.

and half-Spanish, Luca's father was from a strict Catholic family on the Spanish side, and, as Luca explains, was particularly interested in 'the idea of religious iconography'. She also recognized that Miles would appreciate the collection of antique Spanish and Dutch furniture, with its bold shapes and styles. When they finally did unpack the crates and boxes, he was 'like a kid in a candy shop'.

Looking at her father's furniture and pictures in their new setting, Luca admits that it is gratifying to see the collection have 'a new home and a new beginning'. It is impossible to imagine these imposing pieces in a London flat or a smaller house, but in the old rectory the furniture seems right at home.

Holidays to Sri Lanka and the Maldives have left the couple with a love of carved, dark wooden furniture in simple, modern forms, and they have furnished the living room with finds from Lombok, including the mirror, day bed and small tables. The throws, rugs and raffia cushions are all from Ikea, while the embroidered floor cushions are actually grain sacks from Turkey, placed next to Moroccan cushions picked up by Luca on one of her filming projects. The Dutch and Spanish furniture sits comfortably next to more modern finds, such as a 1960s-style lamp.

The Roxbury day bed is a classic piece of design, hand-made in Yorkshire, and appealed to Miles because it is 'more about comfort than style'.

In moving to a Victorian rectory, Miles and Luca wanted to create a home that felt relaxed and welcoming, and were anxious to avoid imposing a formal style. The number of friends and family flocking to the rectory most weekends proves that not only is their house indeed a fabulous weekend retreat, but also that it is the perfect place to unwind.

With a freestanding bath and two huge basins, the bathroom has a glamorous 1930s feel. On the landing, the curved lines of the Indonesian palm-tree sculpture echo the wicker chair from Lombok. The round rattan chair tucked into the corner of one of the bedrooms is from Habitat.

'FOR THE BEDROOMS WE WANTED THAT INDONESIAN FEELING, WITH CRISP, WHITE PILLOWS AND SHEETS AGAINST DARK WOOD.'

Alhambra Abbey

AN IMPOSING GREY STONE HOUSE with turrets and Gothic windows, Hartland Abbey is set within a long, narrow valley in north Devon, a beautiful but isolated spot surrounded by wooded hills leading down to the sea. Peacocks stalk across the gardens calling to each other, and a flock of black sheep graze in the fields beyond. It is a magical setting, and the twelfth-century monks probably felt the same, declaring the setting to be the perfect location for their new abbey.

114

Consecrated in 1160, the abbey was home to the order of St Augustine of Hippo until 1539, when the monastery was dissolved by Henry VIII and given to his Sergeant of the Wine Cellar, William Abbott. The abbey remained relatively untouched until 1704, when one of Abbott's descendants married Paul Orchard, and together they began a dramatic programme of reconstruction. The Orchards' son was quick to tear down most of the original abbey and rebuild it, keen to create a new house in the fashionable neo-Gothic style. The younger Paul Orchard pulled down the Great Hall and abbey chapel in 1755, and razed most of the east side of the main building down to the level of the cloisters on the ground floor. He then constructed three grand reception rooms on the first floor and, above these, a suite of eight bedrooms. Building work was completed in 1779, giving the abbey the appearance it has today.

The Stucley family inherited the house in

1845, and the current occupants, Sir Hugh and Lady Angela Stucley, moved into Hartland in 1996. Portraits and photographs of generations of Stucleys are displayed throughout the house, from medieval paintings to recent wedding snaps. Although open to the public during the summer, Hartland Abbey still feels like a private home rather than a stately pile, and Lady Stucley is adamant that visitors are able to venture into every room in the house.

In the nineteenth century, the family welcomed a new era of design, and the oak panelling on the walls and the ceiling of the dining room were painted with bright, decorative motifs to lift a formerly rather gloomy room. The panels date to the reign of Elizabeth I in the sixteenth century, and were taken from the abbey's Great Hall when it was demolished. Above the panels is a series of murals on linen by Exeter artist, Alfred Beer, commissioned by Sir George Stucley. To ward

Winding paths and terraces, designed by Gertrude Jekyll, lead through woodland gardens of rhododendrons, azaleas, camelias and hydrangeas to the walled gardens.
Previous page: The Stucley family crest can be seen in the nineteenth-century decorative designs on the dining room ceiling.

off the devil, the ceiling includes a painting of the pagan Green Man. The focal point of the dining room is the round nineteenth-century rosewood table, bought for £10 by Lady Sheila Stucley in 1934. Designed by Robert Jupe, it can almost accommodate the entire Stucley family, and extra panels can be added to increase the capacity to twelve, sixteen or twenty diners.

Sir George Stucley's visit in 1862 to the Alhambra Palace in Granada inspired him to redesign the house in a lighter and brighter fashion. He commissioned Sir George Gilbert Scott to design the vaulted Alhambra Corridor, which runs the length of the abbey and was painted and stencilled in vibrant colours. His wife, Lady Elizabeth Stucley, was partial to a more classically English style, and embroidered the coverings for the oak furniture in the drawing room. Sir George's and Lady Elizabeth's initials can be seen throughout the house in the heraldic stained-glass windows, also designed by Alfred Beer.

Set within the original abbey walls, in which niches for candles and crucifixes are still visible, the mint-green library is just off the Alhambra Corridor and is the most complete Regency room in the house. The arched, Gothic-style shelves are lined with leather-bound books, and the rest of the room is hung with ancestral portraits, including a sixteenth-century painting at the far end of the room of a rather severe looking William Abbott and his wife. Elegant portraits by Reynolds of Paul Orchard and his son and daughter-in-law hang above the fireplace.

Today the library remains a favourite family room, with its fantastic collection of books, comfortable chintz sofas and family photographs from the 1930s to the 1950s. With a fire in the grate, it is a cosy place to sit on rainy afternoons or after dinner. The family use the library every evening, and the present Lady Stucley adores watching the sun set over the Atlantic Ocean.

Upstairs, the bedrooms have a light, fresh feel, inspired by the surrounding landscape. White lace panels cover many of the beds, and floral wallpaper brightens up each room. One green-and-white bedroom has French wallpaper with a fern design, chosen to reflect the wild foliage in the grounds of Hartland. Gothic windows surrounded by ivy offer sweeping views over the valley. 'Hartland sleeps thirty,' Lady Stucley explains, 'and the bedrooms range from quite smart to very scruffy. When the house is full, it is bursting

Gothic arches reveal elaborate stencil decoration in the Alhambra Corridor, and a tapestry detail shows heraldic imagery. The corridor is filled with family photographs and portraits, along with a painting of the Antwerp School of Art, attributed to Louis de Caullery.

The entrance has an ornate, Victorian feel with brocade wallpaper and an antique stag's head. The dining-room walls are panelled with Elizabethan oak and hung with family portraits. In the nineteenth century, oak furniture was commissioned for the drawing room, and its coverings were hand-embroidered by the then chatelaine, Lady Elizabeth Stucley.

with grandchildren. We are a huge family, and the house is often stuffed to the rafters.'

A curved wooden staircase leads from the bedrooms downstairs to the Alhambra Corridor and the grand entrance hall. Above the staircase are more family portraits in ornate gilt frames, painted by Richard Buckner. Lit from above by a curved glass cupola, the pictures came from Lady Sheila Stucley's

'WE WANT TO SHARE HARTLAND BECAUSE IT IS SO LOVELY. WHEN TOURISTS VISIT IN THE SUMMER MONTHS, THEY CAN GO INTO EVERY ROOM IN THE HOUSE.'

ancestral home in Exeter. In the main entrance hall, richly-carved wooden panelling and red brocade wallpaper decorate this 'very Victorian' space. The sturdy Gothic front door is secured with a huge brass lock and key.

The grounds at Hartland were first landscaped in the eighteenth century, when hundreds of trees were planted to create the woodland gardens on either side of the valley. The oak avenue in front of the house was laid out in 1750. To escape the devastating gales that blow in from the Atlantic, four walled gardens were built one mile inland. A forest walk through Berry Wood leads down to the sea and Hartland's private beach, with its distinctive grey-and-white striped pebbles. Climbing the steep cliffs on either side reveals views of the dramatic rocky coastline and

the ocean. A tiny cottage overlooks the beach, the only other house for miles around.

In the late nineteenth century, the famous landscape gardener Gertrude Jekyll stayed with Sir Lewis and Lady Stucley at Hartland, and redesigned the paths and terraces throughout the walled gardens. Following World War II, the gardens fell into disrepair, and it was only when Sir Hugh and Lady Angela Stucley inherited the property in the mid-1990s that they were restored. Flowers and vegetables are now tended in the Kitchen Garden, the Walled Garden and the Old Rose Garden, although Sir Hugh admits that 'initially this garden was planted with many roses, but they do not like our climate!'

It is no longer necessary to be a member of either a monastic order or the English aristocracy to visit this lovely abbey. Set within a designated Area of Outstanding Natural Beauty and steeped in local history, Hartland Abbey is an unmissable part of the Devon countryside.

Ranch Retreat

FROM ITS RATHER UNPROMISING start as a C-shaped barn next to a Royal Air Force base in Norfolk has sprung one of the most exciting houses in England. Dynamic design duo Russell Hall and Shaun Clarkson spent two years converting the barn into a fabulous country-house retreat. Leave behind all notions of rose-covered cottages and uptight hotels – Cliff Barns is the ultimate weekend party house.

Russell and Shaun initially wanted to open a bar in Clerkenwell, but after going to several large – and raucously noisy – house parties in the country, the idea for building their own country retreat was born. Their vision for the barn was 'something big and bold', whereas Russell's partner, Petra Boase (see p. 200), was more excited about the 'twinkly lights and chandeliers'. Cliff Barns is an homage to the golden era of *Dallas* ranch style (and a jokey reference to one of the television programme's characters), but also has references to the traditional Scottish hunting lodge and English country cottage.

Perhaps best known for his flamboyant design for the Atlantic Bar & Grill in London, Shaun has also lent his talents to bars and restaurants throughout the capital, including The 10 Rooms, 10 Tokyo Joes, Jerusalem, Pop, Bartok, Denim and The Berkeley Square Café. At Cliff Barns, he was instrumental in choosing the colours and textiles that give the barn its unique look, combining kilims with tartan prints and vintage wallpaper. Using a book titled *Rancho Deluxe* for reference and inspiration, the pair started purchasing interesting pieces at auction before they even owned the building.

As a design team, Shaun and Russell often create a new vision from an antique find, such as the antique stone fountain in the courtyard at Cliff Barns, which has been placed on a contemporary base and surrounded by modern landscaping. In keeping with the house's hunting-lodge aesthetic, a pair of bleached deer antlers overlook the courtyard, complementing the stag's head in the living room and the lighting fixture made from skulls and antlers in the dining room. 'Shaun is very bold in the statements that he makes,' explains Russell, 'and you have to be confident that he knows what he is doing!'

Built on one level, the barn is wrapped around the courtyard, with the living space, dining room and kitchen at one end, and the bedroom suites at the other. The house has five bathrooms and a shower room, and sleeps up to eighteen. with six double bedrooms and a bunkhouse for the children.

Large country houses, particularly English ones, are notorious for their eccentric plumbing and lack of bathrooms. In this house, however, almost every bedroom has its own bathroom, incorporating a freestanding bath or a 'soup-plate' shower. Wet rooms are tiled with slate, and one bathroom has an enormous slate bath that is big enough for two. For a modern take on the four-poster bed, Shaun and Russell have used tree branches and silver birch from the surrounding forests to create dramatic bedrooms. Bedside lamps are from Alfie's Antique Market, in London,

The focal point of the courtyard is a fountain from The Architectural Forum, a salvage shop in London's Essex Road. The deer antlers are from Cobland Farm Antiques, and the round 1950s chairs are Ebay finds. Previous page: A battered case that belonged to Shaun's Aunt Molly sits on top of his old school trunk, and a traditional tartan sofa is covered with an exotic Turkish kilim.

'WE HAD THE IDEA OF A RANCH OR HUNTING LODGE, AND WANTED TO DO SOMETHING DIFFERENT, SOMETHING THAT NO ONE ELSE WAS DOING.'

Victorian wooden chairs have been reupholstered in cowhide from Alma Leather in London's Brick Lane. The local woodyard chopped enormous trees into planks, which were then turned into bookshelves. In the living room and bedrooms, logs are used to produce imaginative side tables.

THE DESIGN IS A FLAMBOYANT TAKE ON RUSTIC: LEATHER CLUB CHAIRS AND COMFY SOFAS SIT IN FRONT OF IMPOSING STONE FIREPLACES AND LIGHTS ARE PERCHED ON TOP OF TREE TRUNKS.

THE FURNITURE COMES FROM A RANGE OF SOURCES; THE
FRENCH-STYLE CHAIRS, FOR EXAMPLE, WERE PICKED UP
FROM A LONDON RESTAURANT THAT HAD CLOSED DOWN.

while the stone walls and vintage wallpaper give rooms a 1970s feel. For that rancho deluxe vibe, each bedroom has Navajo-style blankets and Western saddles – picked up at American auctions – slung over the end of the beds or hanging from the rafters. No room is the same, and one bedroom with a white clapboard roof even contains an antique bathtub.

The surround-sound system is linked to all of the rooms, so that the party can continue throughout the house. Both the living room and the dining room have 'larger-than-life, reclaimed-rock fireplaces', and plenty of leather club chairs and plush sofas for lounging. Almost all of the armchairs and sofas are vintage pieces, reupholstered in tartan prints or cowhide to reinforce the hunting-lodge theme. The floor is covered with an enormous 'oriental' carpet, made in Belgium and bought at auction.

Also acquired in the salerooms, wagon wheels have been wired up as light fixtures, complete with red-fringed lampshades, and hang from the roof beams in the living room. Adding to the dramatic illumination throughout the house are lamps from the 1920s to the 1970s, displayed on tree trunks

cut from the surrounding woodlands.

An industrial-sized kitchen with stainless-steel hobs and ovens can handle anything from Sunday roasts to full English breakfasts. Gingham aprons and a kitchen table with a Cath Kidston tablecloth complete the look. Placed in front of a roaring fire, the mahogany dining table seats eighteen and is adorned with silver candlesticks. The dining chairs around the table frequently get broken during the course of the more wild house parties, and are replaced regularly. Fortunately, an antiques warehouse in nearby Bury St Edmunds ensures that the house receives a steady supply of replacement chairs. To make the most of a stress-free weekend, it is possible to order in food – such as home-made bread, pies and cakes – or to hire a cook to cater for you.

Cliff Barns is the ultimate retreat from urban life. It has all the comforts you would expect from a London hotel – huge beds, luxurious bathrooms, stylish living spaces – but is surrounded by miles of woodland and is within easy reach of the expansive sandy beaches on the north Norfolk coast.

The flour, tea and sugar storage jars are original Hornsea ware from the 1970s. Retro lamps and kitsch sconces add quirky details. Corridors are decorated with vintage wallpaper and antique lamps from Notting Hill, and luxurious Chesterfield sofas sit comfortably with the more ornate Victorian furniture.

CLIFF BARNS IS A QUIRKY HOMAGE TO THE AMERICAN RANCH-STYLE OF *DALLAS*, INCORPORATING SUCH DETAILS AS WESTERN SADDLES, NAVAJO RUGS, WAGON-WHEEL CHANDELIERS AND ARMCHAIRS COVERED IN COWHIDE.

Logs from the nearby woods have been used to create this dramatic bed, framed with lamps from Alfie's Antique Market, in London. The wallpaper, from Trevor Halsham in Park Royal, and the stone walls give the room a 1970s vibe. The corridor leading to the bedrooms has a slate floor and pretty vintage wallpaper.

Weekend Luxury

BABINGTON HOUSE, NEAR FROME, SOMERSET

THE MOMENT NICK JONES DROVE up the sweeping avenue of beech trees to Babington House, he fell in love with both the house and its grounds. It had been a privately owned house until the 1990s, when Nick, who also owns the exclusive Soho House club in London, bought Babington for 'purely selfish reasons'. His idea was to turn it into a new type of country-house hotel, 'somewhere to go at the weekend that feels like home'.

As the same family had lived at Babington for generations, the house was in need of substantial updating. Nick brought in well-known interior designer and former editor of *Elle Decoration*, Ilse Crawford, and was involved with the design from the very beginning. The initial brief was to design a country-house hotel, but Ilse took one look at the Soho House crowd and realized that Babington's future clientele would 'not feel comfortable in a formal hotel environment'. Instead, she approached the project as if it were a family home rather than a country hotel, imagining it as an actual house inhabited by 'a teenage daughter with posters on her walls and a son who is into punk. The parents are away and you can misbehave a little.'

Babington's design evolved in stages as Ilse collected the furniture in bits and pieces on her travels, 'as you would in life'. It is a mixture of traditional English antiques and modern Italian design, together with vintage accessories from other parts of the world. The chandelier over the table in the hallway, for example, was bought while she was on holiday in the south of France.

Believing that country houses should reflect 'the eccentric English architecture of the great stately homes', Nick and Ilse made the conscious decision to keep the layout of the original house. As a result, the bedrooms are larger than rooms of modern proportions, and retain a sense of their history. Ilse had just completed her book *Sensual Home,* and a luxuriously hedonistic approach to design was still fresh in her mind. All that each room needed was 'a really great bath and a really great bed', with walls painted in dark colours 'to create a beautiful, sensual space'. Rather than blowing the budget on the foyer and

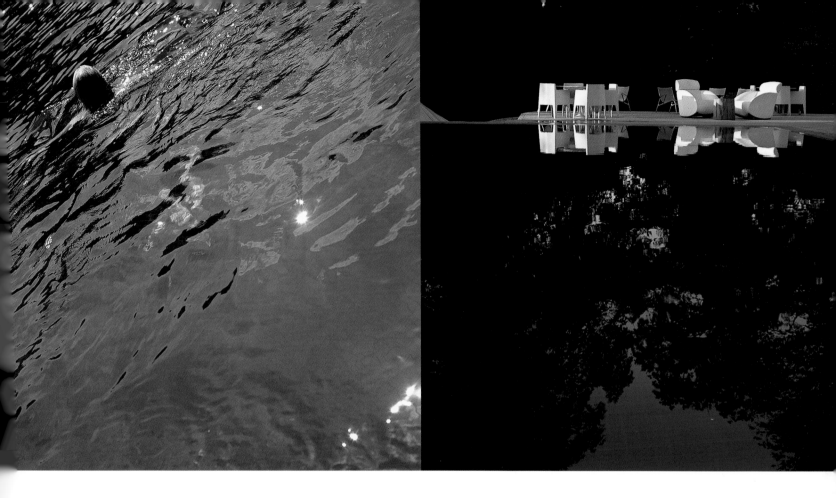

THE SLEEK FURNITURE AND SEXY DESIGN
ANNOUNCE THAT BABINGTON HOUSE IS A NEW
TAKE ON THE TRADITIONAL COUNTRY HOTEL.

Viewed from the avenue of beech trees leading up to the house, Babington looks like a traditional country home, complete with an immaculate croquet lawn.
Previous page: Chairs by Philippe Starck are arranged around hand-made wooden tables in the gardens.

reception areas, Nick and Ilse lavished their attentions on the bedrooms. Ilse wanted to create glamorous bedrooms, moving away from the traditional floral-wallpapered rooms usually found in country hotels. The dark brown bedroom with its silver lamp by Arco (see p. 141) and the deep blue bedroom are two of her favourite rooms in the house.

On the ground floor is the bar, from which guests spill out onto the lawn, dotted with Philippe Starck chairs, in the summer months. It is also where afternoon tea is served, arranged on the counter, and diners perch on

leather barstools or sink into one of the green Chesterfield sofas by George Smith. The bar is one of Ilse's favourite spaces as it is filled with vintage Danish pieces, including chairs reupholstered by Ilse in ponyskin, which sit next to such contemporary Italian pieces as the B&B Italia sofas in dark grey, bright yellow and orange, and Spanish director's chairs. Above the bar are lights designed by local artist Bruce Munroe.

For the dining room, Nick tested various chairs to make sure the most comfortable were chosen, before opting for leather 'Vol Au Vent' chairs from B&B Italia (see p. 139), complemented by dramatic lampshades from Dutch design firm Moooi. The flagstone floor extends out to the terrace, perfectly positioned to provide fabulous views of the lake and the wonderful evening sunsets.

The stables now function as luxury family accommodation, and the cowshed has been converted into a spa. Ilse oversaw the design of the outbuildings, and explains that while within the main house 'each room had its own character, often with interesting mouldings or fireplaces, the outbuildings had been completely overhauled'. Nonetheless, Ilse has managed to produce welcoming living spaces that accommodate young families.

Initially, Nick wanted to knock down the old cowshed and build a slick modern spa in its place, but Ilse persuaded him to leave it standing and to keep the design as a basic shed. The pool extends from inside the shed to an outdoor terrace, and is as warm as a bath. Scattered around the pool are white 'Mumas' chairs by B&B Italia, a contemporary take on the more traditional rocking chair, and silver-mesh loungers by Alias from Twentytwentyone, in London.

When Ilse held her own wedding at Babington in 2000, she put up yurts in the grounds, partly to cope with the English weather and partly to appease her sister, 'who is a hippy'. 'Funny things happen by accident,' Ilse says, 'and Nick did not see the yurts as part of Babington at all. But they are now dotted around the lake and are used for luxurious spa treatments.'

One of Ilse's overriding motivations was to design a hotel in which people felt comfortable and had the 'possibility of evolving'. This aim was realized in the large upstairs room, which was originally intended as a corporate room, 'but nobody was biting'. She persuaded Nick to turn the room into 'a girlie, relaxed, sexy

Hanging upstairs in the Playroom is a classic Eero Aarnio 1960s 'Bubble' chair from Twentytwentyone. Guests congregate in this room and drink martinis until the early hours, before heading downstairs to the Pool Room to smoke cigars and have a game on the full-sized American table covered in purple baize.

AS A WITTY TWIST ON THE TRADITIONAL WOOD-PANELLED DINING ROOM, THE RESTAURANT HAS INSTEAD A WALL OF STACKED LOGS. REFERENCES TO THE WOODLAND THEME ARE PLAYFULLY PICKED UP THROUGHOUT THE HOUSE.

In the bar, the oversized white Anglepoise lamp from Twentytwentyone is over six feet tall and is a reproduction of a 1960s design. The leather 'Vol Au Vent' chairs are from B&B Italia, and the wood-print wallpaper is from Cole & Son.

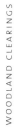
140

space', and now corporate clients can't book it fast enough. Ilse attributes this unexpected success to the fact that she 'gives up the notion of doing things in a prescribed way'.

Setting the standard for all contemporary country hotels, Babington offers the most luxurious – yet relaxed – accommodation, delicious food served throughout the day, and the ultimate pampering spa. Ilse insists that the secret of Babington's phenomenal success is 'having a design that can change', building on the elements that work and rejecting traditional and outdated concepts about country-house hotels.

'I WANTED GLAMOROUS, SEXY AND MODERN BEDROOMS, RATHER THAN THE USUAL "AUNTS' BEDROOMS" WITH THEIR CHINTZY WALLPAPER AND FUSSY DETAILS.'

This corner bedroom is on the first floor of the main house. In-house carpenters made the four-poster bed, and the sculptural wooden legs that support the freestanding bath. The silver lamp is a design classic by Arco from Twentytwentyone, and the silver fan is a modern industrial design.

CLIFFS AND COASTLINES

THROUGHOUT THE CENTURIES, LIVING BY THE SEA — WITH ITS BRACING,

SALTY AIR AND THE SOUND OF SEAGULLS OVERHEAD AND THE WAVES

CRASHING BELOW — HAS HAD A TIMELESS APPEAL. THE ENGLISH SEASIDE IS

A PLACE OF ESCAPE FROM THE BUSY WORLD. WALKING ALONG THE BEACH,

COLLECTING SHELLS AND DRIFTWOOD, EATING COCKLES AND WHELKS

FROM PAPER CONES, AND ENJOYING AN INVIGORATING DIP — REGARDLESS

OF THE WEATHER — ARE SOME OF THE ENDURING BRITISH SEASIDE

PURSUITS. COASTGUARDS' COTTAGES AND LOOKOUTS WERE DESIGNED TO HAVE THE BEST VANTAGE POINTS ALONG THE COAST, AND MANY OF THESE BUILDINGS HAVE BEEN CONVERTED INTO STRIKING AND UNUSUAL HOMES, INCLUDING THOSE AT CUCKMERE HAVEN AND DUNGENESS. LOOKING OUT TOWARDS THE HORIZON, CLIFFTOP HOMES LIKE CLOVELLY COURT AND WEST MILL ENJOY DRAMATIC VIEWS OF THE OCEAN, WHEREAS THE HOTEL TRESANTON OVERLOOKS THE PRETTY FISHING VILLAGE OF ST MAWES.

Clifftop Georgian

WITH NOTHING BETWEEN Clovelly Court and the Atlantic Ocean, the house has one of the best views on the north Devon coast, stretching as far as Lundy Island, forty miles away. Across the parkland, there are views towards Bideford Bay and Exmoor. The Rous family have owned and maintained Clovelly Court and the village of Clovelly since 1738. John Rous, the current owner, has lived here since 1963 and feels that Clovelly Court's appeal lies in its surroundings. The house is north-facing, 'with a bright north light. My favourite view is from the first floor looking across the terraces and seeing the red Cornish rhododendrons in flower in May.'

There has been a house on this clifftop site since the late fourteenth or early fifteenth century, although various alterations over the years have changed the look of the original building. The current incarnation has eleven bedrooms and four reception rooms. In the entrance hallway is a sculpture of John's great-grandfather, born in 1794, who fought in the battle of Waterloo (see p. 150).

In 1943, fire destroyed most of the house's neo-Gothic Georgian wing, which eventually had to be pulled down. Architect Claude Philimore designed the new wing, finished in 1954, which has been christened by John as the 'small marzipan wing'. On the new wing's first floor is the overwhelmingly blue French Wallpaper Room, an impression heightened by the views of the vivid sea and sky beyond. The room is hung with early nineteenth-century hand-painted wallpaper, showing a hunting scene against a blue background. John's grandmother, Christine Hamlyn, acquired the wallpaper from a friend, who loved the design but disliked the subject matter.

Called *Chaise de Campagne*, the design is based on a painting from 1812, and was produced as a wallpaper pattern in the 1830s. There is a fine example of the twelve panels on canvas in the Victoria & Albert Museum, in London, and John remarks drily that the well-known wallpaper firm De Gournay 'has an insipid version in their showroom'. As the room is north-facing, the wallpaper has been protected from fading. The furniture dates from the late eighteenth and early nineteenth centuries, and includes two Georgian torchères from 1789, a nineteenth-century card table and a Regency sofa.

John's favourite room is the Twinnery, which was allocated to his grandmother and her twin sister when they came to stay at Clovelly Court. 'The twins were shoved to one end of the house and told to get on with it', John explains. 'They found it rather bad to begin with and so they started up the rules for the Twinnery. Anyone caught contravening those rules had to pay a fine.'

Christine and her sister invited their neighbour, a librarian called John Fortescue, to be 'king' of the Twinnery, and asked him to write down the rules: 'Nobody shall be admitted to the Twinnery except by invitation – no other visitors shall without special permission be allowed to enter for the purposes of courtship or proposals of marriage or other such selfish, unsocial and exclusive ends.' The Twinnery now contains the library and family chronicles, which are of particular fascination to John. Assembled by Christine, who owned the estate for fifty-two years until her death in 1936, the various scrapbooks record the lives of her family and friends, and the mischief they got up to.

Lawns and terraces surround Clovelly Court, and formerly housed the family's sheep and cattle. Now that the animals have moved on, John says, 'we are gradually civilizing the

Clovelly village perches on a 400-foot cliff; traffic is forbidden and inhabitants used donkeys to transport provisions until the 1990s. Clovelly Court is just a short walk away, set within extensive grounds famed for their Victorian greenhouses and eighteenth-century walled gardens. The clock tower stands at the entrance to the house.

'THE MAIN POINT ABOUT CLOVELLY COURT IS THE VIEWS. THE HOUSE IS NORTH-FACING, LOOKING OUT TO LUNDY ISLAND, WHICH CAN BE REACHED BY BOAT IN AN HOUR.'

JOHN HAS PLACED HIS PANAMA HAT AT A RATHER RAKISH ANGLE ON THE MARBLE BUST OF HIS GREAT-GRANDFATHER, WHO FOUGHT IN THE BATTLE OF WATERLOO.

grounds'. The summer house in the corner of the garden was designed by Rex Whistler, who was also very much involved in the designs for the rest of Clovelly Court. The walled gardens beyond were laid out in the eighteenth century, while the lean-to greenhouses were built in the late nineteenth century. More recent espalier and fan-trained fruit trees line the garden walls that shelter organic vegetables, grown in rotation throughout the year.

Walking through the old Victorian greenhouses, John points out that they are now in better condition than when they were originally built. These glass buildings produce grapes, peaches, nectarines, apricots, melons, Morello cherries, citrus fruits, figs, cucumbers, peppers, chillies, aubergines and tomatoes for the village and its two historic inns, the New Inn and the Red Lion.

John lives and works at Clovelly Court during the week, travelling back up to London at weekends to see his family. In the school holidays, the house is once again filled with children and grandchildren, all enjoying the fabulous views and racing down to the sea.

Standing in the hallway is a marble statue of John's great-grandfather, facing the Gothic grandfather clock and the staircase leading to the French Wallpaper Room. This room is decorated in the characteristic Clovelly blue, and is hung with an 1830s wallpaper design. Rows of bookshelves line the Twinnery, where John's grandmother and her twin sister stayed when they visited in the late nineteenth century.

Sculptor's Studio

ARTIST BRIONY LAWSON SCULPTS in wood, stone and clay, inspired by the landscape around her. Her father, the poet and playwright Ronald Duncan, bought West Mill in Devon in 1937, and Briony, born some years later, has lived there ever since. An extension containing a new gallery and living room has just been finished, with floor-to-ceiling windows on two sides of the living space to take in the sweeping views of the Atlantic Ocean.

Terraces around the house are made from local slate and stone, while the handrails and low, stone walls make use of finds along the high-tide line, including fishing-net floats, rope and whalebones. There is a playful element to the design, apparent in the large lobster mosaic on the outside terrace, made from pebbles and roof tiles by Briony's daughter, Susie, and a slate floor patterned with such games as hopscotch and noughts and crosses. Wooden furniture on the terrace looks as if it was made from driftwood beaten into odd shapes, but was actually crafted by artist Paul Anderson from timber slats, reclaimed from a demolished barn, and bits of oak fences and gateposts.

Briony acknowledges that it was Susie who saw the potential in extending the cottage to create the new gallery, which is now Briony's favourite room in the house. Light streams into this space, highlighting a linen chaise longue and simple wooden chairs, all bought from auctions and junk shops.

Karina, Briony's eldest daughter, recently held her wedding at West Mill, and Briony provided lunch for the one hundred and forty guests, explaining in typically no-nonsense fashion that 'tables are moveable, and we simply put them together'. On a more regular basis, Briony provides meals for groups of art students taking sculpture courses at West Mill. A teetering pile of straw hats on one chair suggests that much of their time is spent outside looking for inspiration in the natural landscape. Depending on their ability and ambition, Briony teaches her students to create sculptures from clay, stone and wood.

Briony's own sculptures can be found in the garden or casually placed throughout the house. The landscape at West Mill is very much an inspiration for her work, and some of her pieces 'originate from the rolling valleys of north Devon', and many images are 'simplified human figures, inspired by a feeling for the natural cycle of life'. Her favourite view of this staggeringly beautiful countryside is from a bench built into a tall bank, looking across the stream to the garden.

The new gallery has a pitched roof with wooden support beams, just as in the main house. Full-length windows extend along both sides of the building. The wide floorboards have been angled across the floor leading to the corner of the room, heightening the sensation that this space continues outside, reaching out towards the ocean. The room is reminiscent of the prow of a ship, and the balcony follows the theme with tensioned nautical wire between the balustrades, rather than slats, so as not to block the view.

On the other side of the atrium, the bedroom has a small window looking into the gallery to make the most of the natural light. All of the walls are painted barley white, with only the wooden window frames and roof beams left exposed. Even the bedroom has a nautical theme, using crisp blue-and-white canvas and cotton throughout. The wardrobe is concealed behind a cream canvas curtain, and the bed is covered with a blue-and-white cotton throw and cushions made by a local upholsterer.

The original cottage and Briony's studio have a warm terracotta floor, worn down over the years by generations of padding feet. Entering the cottage through the front door,

West Mill is hidden at the bottom of a steep, sloping valley in north Devon. Blending in with walls made from local slate and stone are sculptures by Briony and mosaics by her daughter, Susie.
Previous page: In keeping with this natural environment, animal skulls found locally are also displayed on the terraces.

The living room in the original mill cottage has a terracotta floor and wood-beamed ceiling. Against the window is a bronze bust of Briony's father, and arranged along the writing desk are carvings of ferns created by Briony herself. Straw hats piled on an armchair are for the art students who visit West Mill each summer, and spend much of their time outside on the terraces or walking along the clifftop paths.

THE LANDSCAPE AT WEST MILL IS A CONTINUAL INSPIRATION, AND HAS ENCOURAGED GENERATIONS OF ARTISTS AND POETS.

you proceed through the kitchen, warmed by a Rayburn, to the dining room. Just off the dining room is a small living room. Built into the hillside, each room is on a slightly raised level, creating an open-plan space. Logs are piled waist-high next to the living-room fireplace, with cosy armchairs and sofas grouped around it. A tall, thin piece of wood provides a focal point, and is the first woodcarving Briony ever made in 1972.

A short climb up the valley brings the more adventurous walker to a small hut on the coastal path, which Briony's father used as a study in which to write his poetry. In the hope of continuing this tradition, Briony leaves pencils and paper in the hut for anyone who happens to be walking past and is seized by sudden inspiration. It also makes a beautiful spot in which to drink wine and watch the sun set over the Atlantic Ocean.

A wonderfully welcoming atmosphere awaits family, visiting students and a wide collection of friends at West Mill. Sitting with the family in this cosy cottage, it is difficult to imagine a more peaceful or beautiful setting.

THE GALLERY HAS A PITCHED ROOF AND WINDOWS THAT EXTEND FROM THE CORNER ALONG BOTH SIDES OF THE BUILDING. IT IS REMINISCENT OF THE PROW OF A SHIP, POINTING PROUDLY OUT TO SEA.

The new gallery was completed in 2004 and faces towards the ocean. Light streams into the space, highlighting a linen chaise longue and a sculptural terracotta jug. Briony's son-in-law, James, stands at the window next to one of Briony's sculptures, gazing out at the view.

Candlelit Cottage

TO LIVE IN A HOUSE WITH NO heating or electricity, and where the tide almost reaches your front door, requires a certain strength of character. Carolyn McCourt was just twenty-nine when she discovered this remote cottage in Cuckmere Haven, Sussex, and within ten days, the property was hers. Today she lives at Cuckmere with her partner, Cassian, and their little daughter, Li-Chen.

This isolated cottage was built as a coastguard's lookout to prevent smugglers from landing on the Sussex south coast. Apparently, the various occupants over the years were an assertive and determined group when it came to apprehending criminals. Living alone in the cottage, with only a Dalmatian for company, Carolyn had to draw on her own inner resources and training in the martial arts to fend off any potential assailants. Fortunately, within four-and-a-half years of moving in, she met her partner, Cassian Garbett, and the couple now live in the house together with their young daughter. Trained as a woodcarver and furniture-maker, Cassian arrived at the cottage with only a workbench, a suitcase full of clothes and an intricately carved wooden doll's house (see p. 165).

Cassian has helped to shape the look and feel of the cottage. When leaks in the roof filled ten buckets every time it rained, Cassian decided 'it was beyond a joke', and took steps to install a new roof, with tongue-and-groove cladding inside. Having been collecting visually interesting pieces of driftwood, Cassian began to make furniture for the house, starting with a long cabinet in the kitchen for storing utensils, with the bottom three drawers reserved for Li-Chen's toys. Each line of drawers was cut from a single piece of wood, and carved with shells chosen for their 'wonderful names and visual forms of ornamentation' (see p. 164). Cassian has gone on to make stools and flower beds for the outside terrace, as well as an enormous guest bed. He found the huge pieces of wood used to make the bed after a storm in 1999 washed them onto the beach, 'smashed up and lying there like dinosaurs'.

Unusually, given the rather wet British climate, the whole family sleeps outside in a tent from April until October. 'The problem is not the lack of heat,' Carolyn explains, 'but the dampness of our English weather.' They move their pocket-sprung mattress, sheets and pillows to a large canvas tent in the garden, which boasts one of the best views in England. Cosily ensconced in their tent, the family can see the white Seven Sisters cliffs and hear the sound of the sea. 'Waking up in the middle of the night and being able to look out at the stars and hear the oyster catchers and curlews is incredible', Carolyn says. 'The calls of the birds are beautiful, echoing across the beach.'

Carolyn works as a picture restorer,

Approached from the garden, the coastguard's lookout looks like any small cottage. When viewed from the sea, however, its appearance is that of a ramshackle beach hut. Cassian made the terracing from old groynes he picked up in Eastbourne, a long and painstaking process which took five years. In the summer, the family sleeps outside in an old army tent.

163

With no electricity or television, the family have to provide their own entertainment, either whiling away the hours by playing the piano or reading one of the many books collected over the years by Carolyn.

specializing in nineteenth-century paintings and 'anything that needs a bit of care and conservation. I'll clean, patch and retouch, and put paint back where it is missing.' Her work area used to be the front porch, when the land extended out considerably further than it does today. The previous owner changed the porch into a study, and the desk that stands there now originally belonged to him. With a new coat of paint, 'it is a wonderful place for writing'. Carolyn surrounds herself with

drawings and paintings given to her by friends, such as the painting of swallows from a Greek Cypriot, 'who was a real character. I love the freshness of it and the simplicity of the forms.'

With Carolyn's exacting eye for colour, choosing the right shade of blue for the sitting room took some time. 'Certain colours may look fine during the day,' Carolyn says, 'but in the evening by candlelight they can look too strong. White is impossible for me here, I find

it too hard.' Deep blue is used throughout the house, on the walls and around the doors and window-frames. Blue and white also form a checkerboard pattern in the bedroom and porch. 'The colour resonates with me in quite a deep way', she says. 'I can't live in a place without having that colour somewhere; it lifts me. The bedroom was painted in the same colour for a while and I loved it.' With no electricity in the cottage, the couple rely on candles for light, and rapidly work their way

through boxes of 500 at a time from Ikea.

Sofas and armchairs in the living room are from an old house in Normandy that belonged to Carolyn's family. The space is lined with books, which Carolyn has collected since childhood. 'If you are an avid book collector, they are like a facet of yourself,' she explains, 'so I don't think I could get rid of them or give them away.' The wooden fireplace was made by Cassian, and on top of the mantelpiece is a display of small bird skulls and driftwood

found on the beach, next to a picture that Carolyn bought in China almost twenty years ago.

Although the living room – with its rattling windows – is freezing in winter, there are no curtains, due to the potential fire hazard of fabric brushing against the candles' naked flames. Instead, the family gather in front of the fire to keep warm, and even cook over it, placing fish in the burning embers. Carolyn is prosaic about the winter cold, working in front of a portable Calor gas heater when it is especially chilly, or piling on more jumpers.

To make the most of the daylight, the family wakes up early and spends most of the day outside, retreating to the tent at night or lighting candles indoors. 'We are so much more aware of the natural rhythm of the environment', Cassian says. 'Even simple things, like seeing the sun come up over the horizon, and seeing it disappear again at the end of the day. And it is wonderful seeing the moon rise above the Seven Sisters.'

All of the doors and windows in the dining room and bedroom look out to the sea. Hanging on one wall is a wooden fish that came from the Brighton aquarium and was given to Carolyn by a local gallery owner.

Seaside Industrial

A REMOTE COASTGUARD'S TOWER on a shingle beach next to the Dungeness nuclear power station is not everyone's idea of the ideal family home. However, there is much more to Dungeness than its bleak appearance might suggest: it is also a bird sanctuary and home to more than six hundred different types of plants – about one-third of all plants found throughout the UK.

THE FAMILY READ AND RELAX ON THE DECK AND THE BOYS EXPLORE THE OLD LIGHTHOUSE. AS A RETREAT FROM URBAN LONDON LIFE, THIS COASTGUARD'S TOWER ON THE EAST COAST OF KENT IS PERFECT.

Sitting three miles out into the English Channel, this inhospitable piece of land has two lighthouses and around eighty homes scattered along its shore. Most of the houses are made from old rolling stock which were towed off the line to become holiday homes, complete with tongue-and-groove cladding.

The old lighthouse and coastguard's tower are next door to each other, and have not been used for their original purposes since more advanced technology became available. Photographer Peter Marlow was shooting on the beach when he caught sight of a removal van outside the tower, and discovered that the building was up for sale. Living in an old factory in Clerkenwell, Peter and his wife Fiona Naylor were drawn to industrial buildings and could see the tower's potential as a weekend retreat for the family, located an easy one-and-a-half hours from East London.

Having two homes means that there is a clear distinction between working life in London and family time in Dungeness. There is no telephone, computer, or television in the seaside tower, and weekends there are about getting away from it all. Peter, renowned for his spare and elegant landscapes, has always been fond of Dungeness and has photographed here many times.

Fiona runs her own architectural firm, Johnson Naylor, and her design projects have primarily been in London. So the renovation of the coastguard's tower on this windswept coast presented an interesting, if somewhat daunting, challenge. Jutting out into the channel, Dungeness is the most southeasterly point in England and is exposed to some of the country's worst storms. Fiona's priority was to protect the home against gales blowing in across the channel, when rain,

sometimes arriving horizontally, pelts the windows.

Keeping the original steel staircase within the tower, Fiona added a Portuguese limestone floor with underfloor heating throughout. She has since discovered that the stone is porous and is gradually disintegrating outside, but has decided that she quite likes the gently weathered effect.

The steel, wood and stone used throughout the house reflect the materials found along the beach at Dungeness. The wooden kitchen is simple and practical: Fiona designed the oak table, and the chairs with their woven seats are by Hans Wegner. The tower is open-plan, without any doors separating the spaces, even the bathroom. The bedroom is all about warmth and comfort, with a cosy woollen blanket from Scandinavian design store Skandium, and gingham cherry-stone bags

Fishermen's nets and floats are left out to dry on the shingle beach, just along from the old coastguard's tower, now home to Peter and Fiona and their three children. The top-floor viewing area formerly served as the lookout point, but now makes the perfect place to catch up on some reading from the comfort of a vintage armchair.

Fiona designed the floating kitchen units with their stainless-steel work-tops and the oak dining table. The seaside setting is a wonderful place for the children to play and explore.

that are heated in the microwave to serve as hot-water bottles. The bathroom is simply tiled, with shower and taps designed by Arne Jacobsen and bought from Vola, a design firm based in Denmark.

At the top of the house is the viewing

platform, where the coastguard used to sit on watch, twenty-four hours a day. With windows on three sides, his job was to watch the shipping channel and to keep the windows extremely clean! This room is now a peaceful family room, with a wood-burning stove,

HAVING A MUTUAL LOVE OF INDUSTRIAL BUILDINGS, PETER
AND FIONA COULD SEE THE TOWER'S POTENTIAL AS A
FANTASTIC WEEKEND RETREAT FOR THE WHOLE FAMILY.

THE USE OF STEEL, WOOD AND STONE THROUGHOUT THE HOUSE REFLECTS THE MATERIALS FOUND ALONG THE BEACH.

References to the sea are found throughout the house, from the book of tide tables to the life jackets hanging on the wall.
Overleaf: In an effort to keep the house as simple and uncluttered as possible, the bedroom has only a bed covered with a simple grey-and-white blanket from Skandium and a black leather chair from Vitra. The bathroom is decorated with mosaic tiles, and the shower and taps are by Arne Jacobsen for Vola.

mattresses, and beaten-up leather Eames chairs from Vitra. It is a place to sit and read, illuminated by a steel Anglepoise lamp designed by Artemide-Tolomeo.

The kitchen window folds back to create an open living space between the kitchen and the deck. Peter and Fiona take rugs outside to read and relax on the deck, and the children run out to the sea and explore the old lighthouse. As an escape from the stress of urban London life, the coastguard's tower is the perfect weekend retreat for the whole family.

Island Escape

OVERLOOKING SCOLT HEAD ISLAND and harbour, along with a wild nature reserve, Island House boasts one of the most beautiful views in England. When architect Chris Cowper first discovered this derelict Norfolk barn in the 1980s, he instantly recognized its potential, and was inspired to create a wonderful family home.

Island House boasts fantastic views of the island, harbour and nature reserve. The wooden terrace, with its stylish wooden deck chairs, is the perfect place for a cup of tea and to soak in the views.

Chris and his wife Julia first came to this part of the country in 1983 to visit friends who had houses and caravans in the area. 'Long ago, before north Norfolk got the attention of the media,' Chris remembers, 'it was really Cambridge-by-the-sea.' Having fallen for the area and wanting to be close to their friends, the couple began to look around for a house of their own. Fortuitously, the nearby Holkham Estate put a small number of properties on the market. The timing coincided with the end of the 1980s property boom, and 'amazing as it now seems,' Chris says, 'we were the only bidders.'

The couple bought the barn in December 1989, parked a mobile home in the yard, and drove up from Cambridge most weekends to visit the property. They were able to move into the house in December 1992, despite its partially completed state, and then spent a further three years finishing off the interior 'to a fairly basic standard,' Chris admits ruefully, 'through lack of funds.' The couple collaborated on the project with local builder Chris Geering, and 'the main build took about fifteen months,' Chris says, 'but the total project took over six years!'

A desire to avoid the usual bland barn conversion drove the design. Chris felt that it was essential to respect the soaring spaces of

the interior, as well as the original shape of the barn. The first stage was to restore the exterior, which was in terrible condition with no gable ends and no roof structure. The builders began by restoring the masonry, following the lines of the original windows on the ground floor and rebuilding the central openings. All of the external joinery is made from English oak, which Chris bought from a retiring furniture manufacturer.

Moving inside the barn and walking up the stairs, the entire height and length of the original barn is visible. The bridge back to the living room acts as a foil to the sculptural shape of the green stairwell. The large, curved

CHRIS AND JULIA FELT THAT IT WAS ESSENTIAL 'TO RESPECT THE BIG SPACES INSIDE AND THE ORIGINAL FORM OUTSIDE'.

blue wall reflects light from the east and west, and the curving shapes throughout the house were inspired by the sails of passing sailboats in the local harbour. Chris's vision was to create rooms that were fluid in form, 'making a virtue of the way the structure meets the roof and walls. Three dimensionally,' he explains, 'the curve of the wall meets the pitched roof off it, like sails.'

In 2004, the barn was renovated, and Chris insists that the face-lift was 'much more radical than it looks! We sorted out the ground floor in a much better way, so that you can see the view out through the kitchen as soon as you come into the hall.' The plumbing, heating, electricity and lighting were retrofitted, and new floors were laid. Chris is the first to admit that this was 'not a great idea as it was all very expensive, but at least we carried out the work to a good standard in the end. It is nice to see the house as first intended.'

The family's favourite room is the living room, although inevitably they spend most of their time in the kitchen, which was designed by Chris and installed by local furniture-maker Camweavers. It is in the living room that Chris believes the full impact of the house is appreciated, because of 'the journey through the hall and across the bridge to get here, and because of those wonderful, curved walls and large windows that look out onto the balcony'. An added bonus is the incredible view of Scolt Head and the sea, which is 'always changing and always fascinating'.

Furniture throughout the house is a mix of pieces from Ikea, Habitat and The Conran Shop, along with various purchases from local auctions and antiques dealers. The couple tried to avoid the 'jumble-sale approach', but Chris is unsure if they have succeeded. He confides that choosing the right furniture is a 'longer-term project'.

Island House has been a family home for Chris and Julia and their children for fifteen years, a place by the sea to which the whole family can escape. As the family is not able to visit as often as they would like, the house is let for short-term holidays to other families keen to experience the ultimate English seaside holiday.

Nestled on comfortable sofas from The Conran Shop and Habitat in the living room, the family can watch boats sail past to the island. The new kitchen was also designed to have views straight out to sea, and is where the family spend most of their time.

'IT IS ONLY IN THE LIVING ROOM THAT YOU GET THE FULL FEEL OF THE HOUSE, DUE TO THE WONDERFUL, CURVED WALLS AND THE LARGE WINDOWS THAT LOOK OUT ONTO THE BALCONY.'

Cosy bedrooms are filled with furniture and pictures from local auctions and antiques dealers. Sloping ceilings are painted white, and wooden floorboards appear throughout the house. The seaside location is hinted at in the décor, from the sailing boat framed in a window to the circle of pebbles collected from the beach.

Nautical Haven

HOTEL TRESANTON, ST MAWES, CORNWALL

MADE UP OF A CLUSTER of old houses in
St Mawes, Hotel Tresanton is built up over
many different levels and has views of the
estuary leading down to Falmouth and out
to sea. It was one of the best-known and best-
loved hotels in Cornwall in the 1950s and 1960s,
but by the 1990s the hotel was looking tired
and run-down, and only a few of the rooms
remained open. Windows were falling out of
their frames and some of the rooms were being
used for storage. The hotel was offered for sale,
but no-one wanted to buy it.

CHILDREN
FISHING
MUST BE
ACCOMPANIED
BY AN ADULT

One of the West Country's most famous hotels, Hotel Tresanton began life as a yacht club in the 1940s. All of the rooms are sea-facing, looking out toward St Anthony's lighthouse.
Previous page: Mosaic floors throughout the hotel pick up on this maritime theme.

Hotelier Olga Polizzi was introduced to the Tresanton by her husband, William Shawcross, who has a small house next door to the hotel. He had known the hotel in its heyday, often staying there for family holidays as a child. In the post-war 1950s, venturing abroad for holidays was still relatively unusual, and the sleepy Cornish village of St Mawes was a popular destination for well-heeled British tourists, including the Queen Mother. 'William remembered it with the eyes of a child,' Olga

says, 'in a very nostalgic and romantic way.' As a hard-headed business woman and the director of design and build for Rocco Forte Hotels, Olga wasn't sure that she wanted a small hotel in Cornwall.

After much deliberation, Olga bought the Tresanton in 1997 and spent two years restoring and completely redesigning it. The bedrooms on the top floor were a particular problem because the bathrooms were located, rather inconveniently, across the corridor.

Olga's solution was to knock down the back of the hotel and put in a new corridor, ensuring that there was room for a lobby, as well as a bathroom in each room. The period of time from the start of building work to the grand opening was exactly nine months. Olga feels that the new design for the hotel was imposed upon her by the natural surroundings. 'It had to be relaxed, comfortable and light,' she says, 'and in keeping with the local area.'

Cornwall has once again become a popular holiday destination, and Olga believes that the Tresanton has 'done its bit to attract people who had never been to this part of the country before'. She feels that many Britons prefer to holiday in their home country, avoiding the hassles of travelling abroad.

For many years Olga collected drawings by local artist Julian Dyson, and many of his pieces can be seen dotted about the hotel. After Dyson's death in 2003, Olga tried to buy

his studio to keep his work in Cornwall, but was outbid by a gallery in London's Cork Street. Almost all of the paintings and drawings in the hotel are by local artists, although Olga also displays some prized paintings by Patrick Heron and Terry Frost. Wooden models of boats have been picked up from markets and auction houses around the world; one model of a boat built in St Mawes was found in New York and bought back to Cornwall by Olga's brother, Rocco Forte.

Much of the furniture throughout Hotel Tresanton's twenty-nine bedrooms was bought at auction and at antiques fairs, as well as locally in nearby Penzance. Olga's favourite room, Room 3, is so close to the estuary that guests feel as if they are floating above its waters (see p. 194). A desk and antique leather chair from Brussels are positioned in the window to take in the view. The wooden bench at the end of the bed is Indian, the wall lights are from William Yeoward, in London's King's Road, and the wooden light fixtures are from Birmingham firm, Chad Lighting. The bed frame is covered with Belgian linen, and the flooring is fashioned from wide walnut planks.

Each bathroom has an elegant mosaic floor, laid to Olga's design using ceramic tesserae from Italy. She also designed the mosaic flooring throughout the rest of the hotel, collaborating with artist Paul Marks, and is particularly proud of the dining-room floor, which incorporates lines of poetry. In the same room, the white, wooden chairs with their undulating lines belonged to the original 1950s hotel, and were one of the few design elements that Olga was keen to retain.

To promote the feeling of relaxed comfort,

A MOSAIC FLOOR WAS COMMISSIONED TO SOFTEN THE DINING ROOM, USING BLUE AND GREY TONES TO REFLECT THE SEA.

the sitting room has overstuffed sofas from George Smith arranged around a roaring log fire, and there are plenty of board games, newspapers and magazines to occupy guests. Olga could not resist hanging two bronze wall lamps, custom-made in the shape of a stingray, on either side of the sofa (see p. 192).

The cosy lounge on the ground floor has the feel of a sophisticated Italian bar, with its walnut-and-maple striped floor, chic cream armchairs and round tables from The Conran Shop, and is a delightful place in which to have a cocktail before dinner, sitting in front of the fire. The 1930s black lacquered screen is by Italian artist, Leonor Fini, and was picked up at a Christie's auction.

Having opened glamorous hotels across Europe with Rocco, Olga took a risk on her own when she opened Hotel Tresanton in this quiet village. Five years on, the hotel is fully booked nearly every night of the year, with many guests returning for repeat visits. A November visit reveals a clear sea and a fine day for long walks, and in the summer, guests can swim off the beach opposite the hotel in transparent turquoise waters. Olga has not only redefined the English seaside hotel, she has also reinvented the traditional English seaside holiday.

The dining room has floor-to-ceiling windows overlooking the St Mawes estuary. Olga describes what the dining room was like when she first bought the hotel: 'It was quite an ugly shape, with ceilings on different levels and a column in the middle of the space. To unify it all, I added tongue-and-groove cladding and a mosaic floor.'

'THERE IS NO POINT IN DOING A CHIC LONDON HOTEL IN CORNWALL. THE COLOURS OF THE SUN, THE SEA AND THE ROCKS ARE SO STRONG THAT THEY ASK TO BE REPEATED INSIDE.'

The sitting room has a pair of paintings of the Cornish coastline by Hugh Ridge and bronze wall lamps in the shape of stingrays by Paul Verburg. Picking up on the maritime theme, a stone head of Neptune is a feature of the living room.

Olga insisted on buying work from local artists, including the celebrated self-taught artist Julian Dyson, who was born in the village. His seascape hangs in Room 3 and was painted from a sheltered cove in moody blues and greys. The ceramic plate showing Newlyn Harbour is from Newlyn Art Gallery.

'COMFORT HAS TO BE THE FIRST PRIORITY WHEN DESIGNING A HOTEL. THE BEDROOMS MUST BE LUXURIOUSLY COMFORTABLE IN AN UNSELF-CONSCIOUS WAY.'

194

COUNTRY VILLAGE

MEANDERING DOWN COUNTRY LANES LINED WITH TINY COTTAGES,

DISCOVERING THE VILLAGE TEA SHOP AND ITS FRESHLY-BAKED SCONES,

BUYING MILK AND EGGS FROM A CORNER SHOP UNTOUCHED IN THE LAST

CENTURY, AND SPENDING THE EVENING IN THE LOCAL PUB — RURAL VILLAGE

LIFE HAS LOST NONE OF ITS APPEAL. THE LOOK AND FEEL OF EACH VILLAGE

IS UNIQUE TO ITS LOCATION; COTTAGES ARE BUILT WITH GOLDEN

COTSWOLDS STONE IN GLOUCESTERSHIRE, FLINT COBBLES IN NORFOLK,

AND GRANITE IN YORKSHIRE. THESE COUNTRY HOUSES HAVE BEEN REWORKED WITH A MODERN TWIST; THE OUTDATED DÉCOR OF LACE CURTAINS AND CHINTZY WALLPAPER HAS BEEN CONSIGNED TO THE DUSTBIN OF DESIGN AND REPLACED WITH VIVID COLOURS AND UPDATED TEXTILES. A COTTAGE IS FILLED WITH RETRO PIECES, AND A VICTORIAN VILLA IS A RIOT OF COLOUR AND TEXTURE. THE NEW VILLAGE HOME IS ALL ABOUT WARMTH AND COMFORT, WITHOUT SACRIFICING STYLE OR DESIGN.

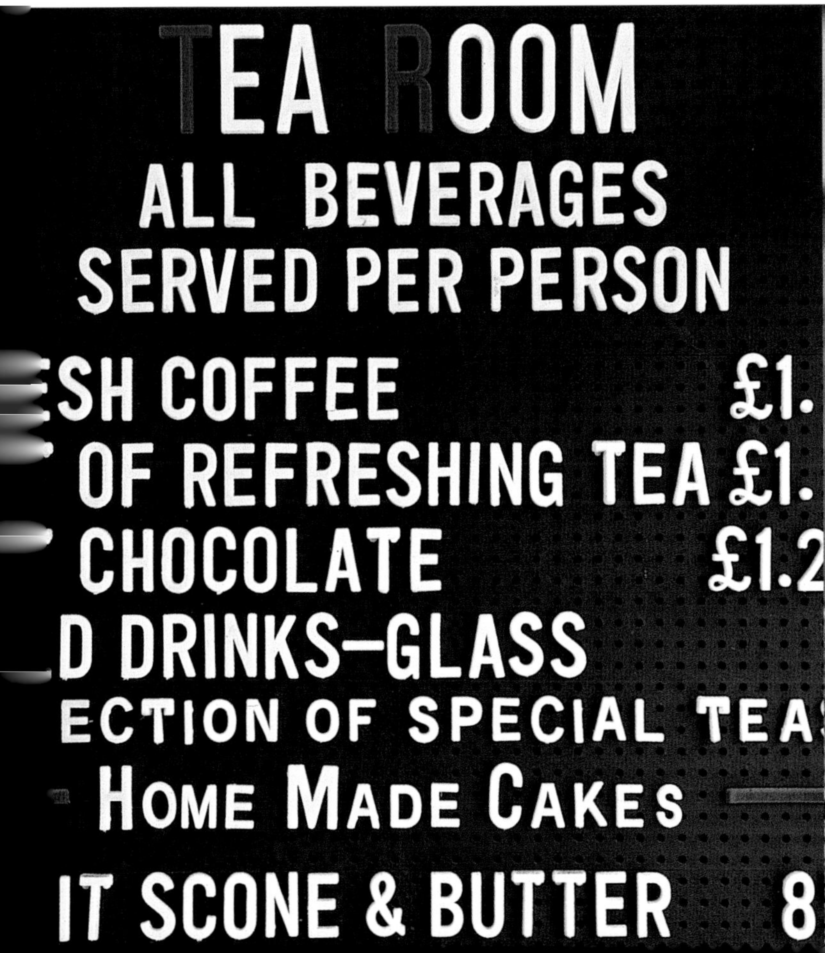

TEA ROOM
ALL BEVERAGES
SERVED PER PERSON
SH COFFEE   £1.
OF REFRESHING TEA £1.
CHOCOLATE   £1.2
D DRINKS—GLASS
ECTION OF SPECIAL TEA
HOME MADE CAKES
IT SCONE & BUTTER   8

Rural Retro

ON THE EDGE OF A SMALL NORFOLK village
and at the end of a narrow dirt track, sits a
tiny cottage with a candy-floss pink front door.
Apple blossom blows gently across the garden
as Petra Boase, with baby Florence in her arms,
comes out to greet us. To jaded and envious
Londoners, this seems like the most idyllic life.

The family lives in a small two-up, two-down flint cottage with a pink front door. In the garden, the table is laid for tea with a vintage tablecloth, enamel teapot and a retro sugar bowl, cream jug and mugs.

On a warm spring day, we sit in the garden drinking tea from 1960s cups and eating an especially delicious chocolate-biscuit cake. A selection from Petra's collection of vintage fabrics hangs on the washing line, blowing merrily in the breeze.

It may seem surprising that Petra, one of London's most creative textile designers, made the move to the country at all. Her partner Russell Hall was also very much part of the creative London scene, working as a set designer for MTV and collaborating with interior designer Shaun Clarkson (see p. 122). Petra and Russell made their move gradually, realizing that Norfolk would be a wonderful

place in which to run their respective businesses and to raise a family.

Petra has built a huge sage-green shed in the garden, where she makes hand-made cards, boxes and photograph albums for design stores around the world, including The Conran Shop and Liberty. There is a huge demand for her work, but for now she is happy to keep her business on a small scale and to collaborate with the local Women's Institute on a new range of fluorescent-pink stripy teddy bears! Local towns have been hugely inspirational for both Petra and Russell, where they find fantastic charity-shop bargains and treasures in the local salerooms. Petra

specializes in vintage fabric, which she picks up for around £2 a piece, while Russell has an unerring eye for furniture.

Walking through the front door, it is obvious that this is not your typical chintz-filled country cottage. A collection of desirably fashionable scarves by Petra's college friend Jo Gordon hangs behind the door, and a pair of sparkly heels stand to attention on the floor. The kitchen table is made from an old door, as the couple could not find a table big enough for all their friends (although they are now thinking about getting a proper one made). This makeshift table is covered with a practical Cath Kidston oilcloth.

The living room best reflects Petra and Russell's individual characters, with its mix of old and new finds. Vintage cushions are scattered haphazardly across a black leather Habitat sofa against the wall. Nearby, a 1950s wooden coffee table has two 1960s-style

SITTING IN PETRA'S LOVELY GARDEN, DRINKING TEA ON A WARM SPRING DAY, IS A HEAVENLY WAY TO SPEND AN AFTERNOON.

The bathroom has a pink theme, right down to the choice of colour for the Chinese paper lantern. A suitably pink candle rests in an antique enamel candle holder that doubles as a soap dish. Mint-green tongue-and-groove shelving holds treasured books and ceramics and pressed-glass candlesticks.

leatherette swivel chairs on either side of it. The Art Deco armchair, bought for £4 at a local auction, was given a new lease of life by reupholstering it in a bright, vintage fabric. The small sofa against the wall has also been recovered, this time using a 1970s pattern from Heal's.

Renovating their cottage started out as a part-time project, with Petra and Russell driving up from London at weekends to strip wallpaper and knock through walls. They

eventually moved into the house when it was still a bare shell, cooking on a camp stove and improvising for furniture. Keeping the design simple, the couple decided that the next stage was to install underfloor heating, wooden floorboards, white walls and a basic kitchen from Ikea. A white, wooden staircase leads to the bedrooms and bathroom off a narrow corridor papered with dusky-blue Finnish wallpaper, printed with delicate Japanese white blossom.

AN ANTIQUE TIN BOX FULL OF LOGS FOR THE FIRE IS READY
FOR COLD WINTER NIGHTS. ABOVE THE SOFA, A FRAMED
1970s 'FRESH MILK' TEA TOWEL HANGS NEXT TO A
CONTEMPORARY PIGEON LIGHT FROM THE CONRAN SHOP.

A girlie haven, the upstairs bathroom has a 'quirky knick-knack shrine' at the end of the bath, filled with Petra's treasures. She customized her trinket cabinet by adding a mirror at the back, and painting it a glossy turquoise. A hot-pink Chinese paper lantern hangs from the ceiling and a woven plastic pink-and-white 1950s chair, an 'impulse Ebay purchase', sits next to the bath (see p. 205).

The bedroom combines Petra's love of traditional British craft with Russell's American retro style. Their bed is covered with pretty floral sheets and pillowcases and a multicoloured crocheted bedcover, while on top of the dressing table is a 1960s Miami lamp with a pirouetting dancer and parchment lampshade. The windows are hung with 1920s glazed-cotton curtains.

Opposite the master bedroom is the nursery, a vintage haven for a seven-month-old baby! Decorated in delicate, muted colours, the room has walls papered with mint-and-white polka dots and a collection of vintage quilts and eiderdowns on the bed. The baby's clothes are stored in a chest of drawers from British design company, Ercol.

Life in Norfolk is very much that of a work in progress, not least because Petra and Russell are still renovating another project, their beach hut in Old Hunstanton, which they are planning to paint in stripes of Petra's signature candy-floss pink and white. Liking the 1960s-vibe of the hut, they will leave the faux wood-panelled interior and simply add vintage curtains and cushions. Inspired by their local surroundings, Russell and Petra have created a new Norfolk style of their own.

Looking toward baby Florence's room, the doorway is framed by Japanese wallpaper, while the nursery is decorated with fresh, light colours and old paisley prints. The round nursing chair has been covered with vintage scraps of fabric, including a farmyard print.

THE BEDROOM IS AN HOMAGE TO TRADITIONAL BRITISH CRAFT AND AMERICAN RETRO STYLE WITH PRETTY FLORALS AND A CROCHETED BEDCOVER.

Theatrical Spectacle

MOVING TO THE DEPTHS OF north Norfolk in 1989 to pursue successful careers as an architect and a fashion designer, Tom and Henrietta Faire found that they missed going to the theatre. Undaunted, and being practical souls, they decided to build their own. The result is a versatile space that works as both a theatre and dining room-cum-drawing room. The Balcony Film & Arts Club was born and is now an essential part of Norfolk life.

Built around 1840, the couple's home, Stokers, was once the old harbour master's cottage. Having decided to press ahead with the new project, Tom began drawing up plans to extend the cottage into the garden to create a small theatre space. Working on a site in London at around the same time, Tom began chatting to a builder who told him that rows of tiered seating from the Royal Court Theatre in Sloane Square had been thrown out. He managed to rescue eighteen seats, and reupholstered them in traditional red velvet.

Work began in July 1994 and was completed in April 1998, just in time for Tom's fortieth birthday. To encourage paying guests, the couple knew that they needed to recreate the authentic movie-going experience, and installed a 35mm film projector, a 16-foot cinema screen (which disappears into the ceiling), and a surround-sound system.

With the help of hydraulic lifts, the Royal Court seating sinks beneath the drawing room floorboards, and re-emerges with the flick of a switch and some levering and winching. Up to thirty-six people can be accommodated in the theatre. 'There are eighteen people on the theatre seats,' Henrietta explains, 'four on the lovers' seats, and fourteen more on other sofas, armchairs and rocking chairs!'

While Tom worked on the architectural design of the theatre, Henrietta applied her own skills as a dressmaker to the interior. To block out the light from the kitchen, she made a wall-hanging from burgundy taffeta edged in gold rope, with 'The Balcony Theatre' hand-painted in gold. She also whipped up curtains from 36 metres (118 feet!) of red-and-gold Mulberry chenille, woven in Florence, and added gold fringing for good measure. In keeping with these colours, the sofa from The Conran Shop is covered with a burgundy-and-green brocade. Forty-eight seat cushions, also stitched by Henrietta, ensure the comfort of their visitors.

The Balcony Theatre also hosts concerts and plays in the round for up to fifty guests, but 'this is a squish', admits Henrietta.

A HIGHLIGHT AT THE BALCONY THEATRE IS WHEN PIANIST NEIL BRAND ACCOMPANIES SILENT FILM CLASSICS.

The Steinway piano is in constant use for both classical music and jazz concerts, not to mention when top silent-movie pianist Neil Brand accompanies Buster Keaton and Harold Lloyd classics from the 1920s.

During term-time, cinema screenings of art-house films from around the world are held every Friday and Saturday, and are often followed by talks and question-and-answer sessions with well-known directors, producers and actors. On Saturday evenings, Tom and Henrietta frequently cook dinner for up to thirty theatre-goers, specially choosing the food and drink to reflect the nationality, whether Tibetan or Argentinian, of the film.

Large numbers of people can be catered for in the kitchen, which has an enormous Lacanche range cooker at one end and a vast

Tom and Henrietta hand-picked the flint cobbles from the shingle yard in Wells-Next-the-Sea, just down the road. For the garden, they commissioned a mosaic table to their design, using subtle tones of blue, gold, red and yellow. Many Norfolk houses have sheltered courtyard gardens to protect plants from the cold north wind. The natural palette of the garden echoes the soft colours of the cobbles. Tom's old bicycle has been restored and is propped up against the front of the house.

Hanging above the kitchen table is a rusty chandelier that Henrietta picked up from a Fakenham auction, where it was languishing in an old trunk. Favourite tea cups and ceramics, such as these blue-rimmed cups from Casa Fina in Covent Garden, are displayed on the apple-green French baker's stand. A Malaysian puppet hangs from the dish-rack, while Mexican papier-mâché fruit, together with the more edible kind, is displayed in a Moroccan ceramic bowl.

French sink under the window. Malaysian masks and puppets from Venice and Prague are arranged against the chalky-pink walls, continuing the theatrical theme. The scrubbed-pine table occupies the centre of the room and was made locally at The Granary, in Snettisham. It can comfortably seat up to twelve people on chairs covered with embroidered cushions made by Tom's grandmother. Unfortunately, the family can only use their dining room in the school holidays when the theatre seats are packed away, but the stage-cum-drawing room is in constant use.

When the cottage was converted, the hayloft became a bedroom for the couple's daughter, Olivia. This loft-style space also houses the film projector, and every weekend is taken over as the projection room for a few hours. For their son's bedroom, Henrietta

bought second-hand wooden bunk-beds for £10, which she painted with 'a dark green base coat, a layer of shellac and a bright viridian green topcoat'. She used Chris Mowe's hand-made earth pigment paints, which were then rubbed down and polished. The bathroom is tucked under the sloping roof, and there is room for a freestanding bath. In the master bedroom, the eighteenth-century bed is housed in an alcove surrounded by murals of wild beasts inspired by ancient Egyptian wall paintings and painted by local artist, Mary MacCarthy. Henrietta's brother, Hugh Webster, is also a talented painter, and his seascapes of the east coast can be seen throughout the house.

Being film enthusiasts – Tom's favourite film is Georg Wilhelm Pabst's *Pandora's Box* and Henrietta's is Ingmar Bergman's *Fanny and Alexander* – does not prevent the family

from enjoying the great outdoors. They are
never happier than when sailing around the
coast in their Norfolk Gypsy sailboat, *Betsy*,
or gathering chestnuts in Holkham Park
in the autumn.

FROM MALAYSIAN PUPPETS TO MOROCCAN CERAMICS,
FRENCH BAKER'S STANDS TO MEXICAN PAPIER-MÂCHÉ
FRUIT, SUCH DETAILS CREATE A FAMILY KITCHEN THAT
IS WARM AND INVITING.

Television presenter Kevin McCloud designed the chandelier and sconces, and the large kilim was bought in Fez thirty years ago. Curved shutters are painted by Charles Lant with scenes inspired by Jean Genet's play *Le Balcon*, on which Tom and Henrietta based the name of their own theatre.

IN 1998, TOM AND HENRIETTA FULFILLED A LONG-HELD DREAM OF BUILDING A SMALL THEATRE IN WHICH TO SHOW CONTEMPORARY AND ART-HOUSE FILMS, HOST CONCERTS AND PERFORM PLAYS.

Rich Tapestry

AS TEXTILE DESIGNERS RENOWNED for their bold sense of colour and design, Brandon Mably and Kaffe Fassett were drawn to the Sussex south coast, to the bright light and vivid hues of the seaside towns. Kaffe has designed collections for Missoni and Designers Guild, and is considered a leader in the world of colour and textiles. Knitwear designer Brandon is studio manager at Kaffe Fassett Studio and teaches workshops around the world.

This tropical garden reflects the mild climate of the south coast and hints at the vivid colours within the house. The dense green foliage of the driveway is echoed in the hand-painted chinoiserie wallpaper in the dining room. The owners' artistic sensibilities are apparent in the sculptures, mosaics and plants throughout the garden.

Finding their home in Rye too cramped and dark, Brandon and Kaffe began searching for a house with lots of space and lots of light. Feeling that Brighton had lost some of its character in recent years, they looked further east along the coast. Upon coming across The Hollies, a large lavender-blue Victorian villa just outside Hastings, the couple were not initially impressed, ranking the house 'at the bottom of the pile'. But when Brandon walked into the living room 'late in the afternoon in August, with the sun streaming in through the two bay windows', he knew that this was the house they had been looking for. They moved in a mere one month later, the day after the

events of September 11, 2001.

From these inauspicious beginnings, The Hollies has become a much-loved family home. Their busy lives mean that Brandon and Kaffe only use the house at weekends, and as it has plenty of rooms, Brandon's mother, Yvonne, and sister, Belinda, also make their home there. When she first saw the house, Yvonne described it as 'very magnolia and a bit dour', but she remembers that Kaffe and Brandon loved the house from the moment they purchased it, 'the floors, the light, and the whole feel of the place'.

Arriving at The Hollies, set within its luxuriant garden, visitors are immediately

aware of the couple's love of colour and texture. Inside the house, the huge living room, with its 13-foot-high ceilings, is flooded with light from the two bay windows. At the far end of the pale yellow room is a mural painted in oils, which Kaffe worked over with acrylics. The couple's artistic touch can be seen throughout the room, from the curtains with their pastel handkerchief-pattern patchwork and needlepoint pelmets in yellow and cream, to the needlepoint-covered chairs. Also in the room, the peony-covered armchair is decorated with needlepoint by Yvonne and Belinda. Most of the furniture was found in the antiques shops in Rye and Hastings.

The mint-green dining room opposite the living room is a much smaller space, perfect for the 'intimate and nostalgic' dinner parties that the couple enjoy hosting. Hanging hand-painted chinoiserie wallpaper would have been far too expensive, so Kaffe painted the

KAFFE CAME DOWN TO THE HOLLIES EVERY WEEKEND OVER THREE MONTHS TO PAINT THE DELICATE CHINOISERIE DESIGN ON THE DINING ROOM WALLS.

designs himself. Once it was finished, Brandon and Kaffe visited Murano, the centre of the Venetian glass industry since the thirteenth century, to commission a hand-blown glass chandelier to complete this exquisite room. And, just in case they were in need of any further inspiration, the couple were guests at the Missoni apartment in Venice!

Living areas are on the ground floor, while the bedrooms lead off from a corridor on the first floor. Hanging in the master bedroom is a quilt from Germany. It is made up of scraps from men's suits, some of which were worn at Auschwitz, and its severe colours and heavy bars and stripes are intended to symbolize the falling of the Berlin Wall.

Belinda's bedroom has magenta walls and a curved bateau lit, 'a huge boat of a bed'. It is an utterly feminine and romantic room, perfectly in keeping with the sensual design of the house. Covering the bed are more examples of Belinda's needlepoint, inspired by

Light floods into the living room, which is the perfect showcase for Brandon and Kaffe's work, including the patchwork curtains and mural designs. Needlepoint cushions and tapestries have been worked on by the whole family.

Brandon's mother, Yvonne, is shown at work knitting yet another beautiful design. Examples of Yvonne and Belinda's needlepoint appear throughout the house.

Kaffe's designs, and a striped, knitted shawl by Missoni for *Vogue*. Just down the corridor is a bedroom decorated with Indian wedding saris and an old patchwork quilt made from scraps of cotton and velvet. There is another quilt underneath, which is incredibly heavy due to both the intricate embroidery and to the pieces of mirror woven into the design by Indian gypsies.

Most of Brandon's time at The Hollies is spent in the kitchen and breakfast room, and particularly the garden, which he tends with Yvonne's help. Brandon is proud of his 'tropical garden, which shows you what the climate is like'. Having a house near the sea has helped keep him sane, Brandon admits, as he can take the time 'to breathe the wind and air'. Kaffe and Brandon have created an oasis of colour and calm to return to again and again from their travels around the world, and to escape to from the constant hive of activity that is their London studio.

THE FEMININE MOOD OF THE HOUSE IS ECHOED IN THE RICH, WARM TONES OF THE BEDROOM AND THE CURVED LINES OF THE BATEAU LIT.

Cornish Grandeur

FOWEY HALL, FOWEY, CORNWALL

FOR NEARLY THIRTY YEARS, Fowey Hall was filled with ramblers in sensible boots sleeping six to a room, courtesy of the Countrywide Holiday Association. It was a rather spartan affair, with a sink in each room and a shower block at the end of the corridor. Breakfast was at 8 a.m. sharp, with guests taking it in turns to do the washing up. Ramblers were provided with packed lunches, returning in the evening for a meal around a long, communal table of such hearty fare as roast lamb followed by Black Forest gâteau.

Luxury Family Hotels bought Fowey Hall in 1996, when its interior had been reduced to a few worn-out beds and some chipped sinks. There were no chairs, lampshades, or paintings to soften the rather neglected look of the once grand building. A year and £1.5 million later, Fowey Hall arose from the ashes as a smart country hotel. Tim Brocklebank, general manager and one of the current owners, remembers the renovation process: 'On the ground floor the wooden panelling and the flooring remained, and we just put down some rugs. In cases when we opened up the panelling, we would find the original moulding underneath.'

Fowey Hall opened its doors to the public in the summer of 1997, and has been through some difficult times since. The hotel's fortunes took a turn for the better when, as Tim recalls, 'the whole Eden and Cornwall thing really began to accelerate and we rode the wave. It was fantastic and we haven't looked back.' The award-winning Eden Project and television chef, cookery writer and West Country native Rick Stein have focused attention on the area, although Cornwall 'has always been a very special place'.

Tim takes a pragmatic view regarding the

hall's contents. 'Nothing in the hotel is particularly expensive,' he explains, 'because it is a family friendly hotel and children have the run of the place. Priceless antiques would just get knocked over.' A baby grand piano in the entrance hall was dropped when it was brought in, and consequently 'doesn't work

FOWEY HAS INSPIRED GENERATIONS OF WRITERS, FROM DAPHNE DU MAURIER TO KENNETH GRAHAME.

very well', Tim remarks cheerfully. 'But the kids can have a bash and enjoy it.'

Fowey Hall oozes a charm and elegance that is apparent from the moment you step into the entrance hall, with its log fire and vintage chandelier twinkling overhead. According to Tim, it is all a sophisticated illusion; the elegant bust silhouetted in the window, for example, was 'bought in a junk shop'. He also put up a large number of mirrors, 'because we like lots of light and reflection', and chose a combination of 'old mirrors with antique glass, and quite simple

This hotel on the south Cornish coast overlooks the pretty fishing village of Fowey. The sandy cove at Readymoney is a short walk from the hotel. Previous page: One of the arms has already fallen off the grand candelabra in the drawing room, a detail in keeping with the faded grandeur of Fowey Hall.

mirrors sprayed with gold paint'.

The drawing room has a grand feel to it, with the original marble fireplace, parquet flooring and elaborate plaster mouldings. An antique chandelier with a three-foot drop came from a country house in Exeter. Vintage bamboo rattan furniture is set off by brown-and-gold cushions of velvet and brocade. 'Much of the furniture was in a very poor state,' Tim explains, 'but we have a master craftsman who repairs and reupholsters pieces

that need attention.' The candelabra is made up of two pieces joined together, although Tim admits that one of the arms has already been lost. With dripping wax candles and a roaring fire, the house is more about atmosphere than being a showcase for precious furniture.

Sir Charles Hanson was the original owner of Fowey Hall. Making his fortune in the lumber trade in Canada, he returned to Cornwall to build his grand house in 1899, just across the water from his boyhood village of

Polruan. A flamboyant character, Hanson
developed a love of the ornate, Italian palazzo
style, evident in the grand living spaces
decorated with Baroque plasterwork,
chandeliers and marble fireplaces. The fine
wooden panelling on the ground floor was
made in Canada and shipped over to England.

A Canaletto painting hung at one time
above the mantelpiece in the dining room, but
was sold by the Hanson family. The space is
still a gracious room, seating up to fifty guests

The drawing room and dining
room still have their original
nineteenth-century wooden
panelling and mouldings. The
furniture is a mix of
contemporary and antique,
covered in rich velvets and
brocade.

on elegant, curved wooden chairs and lit by French Baroque lamps with silk shades and crystal drops. The rooms on the ground floor, including the library and drawing room, have all been returned to their original uses.

Fowey Hall is a bit like the house of an eccentric great-aunt, with its faded grandeur and family feel. Tim stresses that 'there is an informality that I want to maintain here'. Guests are predominantly young families who love the laid-back atmosphere of the hotel, as well as the feeling of being looked after.

Filled with nineteenth-century French furniture and antique tapestries, the suite at Fowey has an opulent feel. The antique bed has been upholstered in deep red velvet, and rich brocades cover the sofa and armchair, creating a warm and inviting room.

THE LITTLE TOWN LAY IN A SHELTERED WAY

ENLACED IN THE ARMS OF HER WOODED SHORES,

A DOZING FORT ON HER RAISED RIGHT FIST,

A CROSS ON THE BONES OF A DROWNED LEFT WRIST,

COCOONED FROM THE WINDS AND WARS.

AN EXTRACT FROM THE 18TH-CENTURY POEM, *THE FERRYMAN*, DESCRIBING FOWEY

CORNISH GRANDEUR

FARM

ENGLAND'S COUNTRYSIDE IS A PATCHWORK OF FIELDS AND FARMS, STRETCHING ACROSS THE LANDSCAPE. ANCIENT STONE FARMHOUSES AND MORE MODERN BUILDINGS ARE SURROUNDED BY MEADOWS AND HEDGEROWS AND FIELDS OF WHEAT AND BARLEY. FARMS ARE AT THE HEART OF RURAL COMMUNITIES, PROVIDING SEASONAL FRUIT AND VEGETABLES, FRESH MILK AND EGGS TO THE SURROUNDING AREAS. OLD FARMHOUSES ARE NOW POPULAR FAMILY HOMES, AND THE NEW INHABITANTS

CONTINUE THIS RURAL WAY OF LIFE, WITH CHICKENS IN THE YARD AND SHEEP GRAZING IN THE NEARBY FIELDS. THE FARMS IN THIS CHAPTER ARE INHABITED BY A NEW BREED OF COUNTRY DWELLER, TAKING TRADITIONAL BUILDINGS AND GIVING THEM A NEW PURPOSE. SHEEPDROVE FARM IN WILTSHIRE IS COMMITTED TO RESTORING BIRDS AND WILDLIFE TO THE LOCAL COUNTRYSIDE, CLIVE BOWEN HAS CONVERTED HIS DEVON FARMHOUSE INTO A STUDIO AND POTTERY, AND COWLEY MANOR IS NOW AN ELEGANT COUNTRY HOTEL.

Rustic Reclaimed

DAVID AND GINNY MURRAY bought a derelict cow byre and two acres of land in 1988, and spent ten years converting it into a family home. Building the house was a creative process, with furniture-maker David painting and sketching his ideas 'until it looked right'. When the couple purchased the byre, only a few walls of it were left and the whole space was completely open to the sky. Initially, Peter wanted to live in one house with Ginny while the children lived in the other, but admits wistfully that 'it has not worked out like that'.

The cow byre is in the same Cotswolds valley where David was born. His father was a farmer, and David always imagined that he would follow in his footsteps, but gradually realized that farming today was a much tougher prospect. 'I was brought up as a farmer,' he says, 'and from my own house I can see the house in which my father and I were born. It is the only other house around for miles.'

Throughout the restoration, David was living in a cottage on the property and 'farming this entire valley of 700 sheep and 100 head of cattle'. Things reached a crisis point when David's father died, and he was left managing the farm on his own. Realizing the physical impossibility of doing both, David had to choose whether to finish the restoration project or to carry on farming. He reached a compromise by continuing to farm the fifty acres around the byre, but does not rely on the results for a living.

Like many frustrated homeowners, David admits that he 'couldn't stand to have any builders', so he took the more unusual step of involving the local community of travellers. The resident workforce turned up in covered wagons and stayed on site, employing their skill at a somewhat slow and measured pace. As a result, the project took ten years to complete.

Flagstones from the nearby church's original floor feature in the byre, and each doorway and window frame is unique, being either an original piece of architectural salvage, or hand-made by David from reclaimed wood. The kitchen door is made from ancient oak planks on one side and old coffin boards on the other, and is draught-proofed with a canvas lining between the two. David made the table, chairs and kitchen units, above which are shelves lined with old teapots, vintage glasses, and jars from the 1950s for sugar and coffee. A reclaimed Aga completes the look.

The treads on the stairs are solid blocks of green oak, and so thick that they took five years to dry out. It was only then that David was able to add the banister, made from a single yew tree, without danger of the wood cracking. The upstairs consists of the master bedroom, a bathroom and two children's bedrooms. A freestanding reclaimed bath with vintage taps has pride of place in the bathroom, with views of the valley on three sides. Twin circular basins were rescued from a monastery.

Creature comforts include a log fire in the living room, and cosy sofas and armchairs piled high with cushions and throws. David lowered an old door onto the fireplace to create the arched surround. A guitar leaning

When David and Ginny bought the ruined byre in 1988, the only materials at their disposal with which to rebuild the house were a pile of oak planks, a box of salvaged metal latches, and a stack of old stone tiles. A leather satchel acts as an informal post box by the front door.

THE WORK WAS CARRIED OUT BY LOCAL TRAVELLERS, RATHER THAN BUILDERS, WHO STAYED ON SITE AND COMPLETED THE RENOVATIONS WITH SKILL AND DEDICATION.

David's skills as a carpenter were used to build the main staircase from solid pieces of oak, and to design and build the table and chairs. He also used an old stile to create the arch over the front door.

against the wall is often brought out for informal gatherings with friends and family. Next door is the music room, with a piano on which singer-songwriter Ginny and their two daughters practise. Underfloor heating throughout the house warms up the flagstone floors.

Only a few family heirlooms were rescued from David's childhood home, among them some old wooden chests found in a barn, where they had been stored since 1925 when the family moved house. David admits that they have nearly rotted away, but he has kept 'all the bits that have fallen off' in the hopes of one day restoring them. Now in demand as a furniture-maker, David is relishing his chosen career. 'You have to reinvent yourself when living in the countryside,' he explains, 'because the old structure of farming, which used to support a way of life for a whole community, is no longer there.'

WHETHER MADE BY HAND OR RECLAIMED FROM A SALVAGE
YARD, EACH DOORWAY AND WINDOW FRAME IS UNIQUE,
AND ADDS TO THE RICH CHARACTER OF THE HOUSE.

The stone walls and cobbled floors were painstakingly built by hand, using golden Cotswolds stone from old buildings and reclamation yards. Oak floorboards, mullioned windows and the wooden ceiling beam were architectural salvage finds.

THE BATHROOM WITH ITS FREESTANDING BATH AND COMFORTABLE SEATING HAS BEAUTIFUL VIEWS OF THE COTSWOLDS VALLEY ON THREE SIDES.

Farmhouse Organic

PETER AND JULIET KINDERSLEY, founders of
the hugely successful publishing firm Dorling
Kindersley, bought a derelict Berkshire
farmhouse in 1970 in order 'to practise our
dream of self-sufficiency'. When they first
purchased the house, Sheepdrove Farm had
four rooms downstairs and three rooms above,
but no electricity. Consequently, living at
Sheepdrove was a challenge from the start.

From early on, Peter and Juliet had a clear vision of what their home would look like, despite its rather unpromising appearance. Juliet admits that the house's 1960s pebble-dashed exterior did not help matters. Inspiration came whilst driving to their son's school in South Molton in Devon, when the couple came across four intriguing Gothic windows in an architectural antiques shop. Although they readily admit that they bought the windows 'for no good reason', those windows quickly became the style guide for the rest of the house.

Built during the 1850s, the original farmhouse now forms the central part of Sheepdrove, which Juliet refers to as the 'tube train' because of its long, narrow construction. Peter and Juliet added a hallway and kitchen at one end, and a sitting room at the other, with the result that the new house resembles the shape of a cross, a form suitably in keeping with its Gothic theme.

Despite working with both an architect and a local builder, Peter and Juliet did much of the work themselves, drawing on their renovation experience in London to accomplish the plastering and install the central heating. With the house only connected to mains electricity in 1995, for the first ten years the family generated their own power with a windmill, then a gas-fired Renault generator, and finally a Lister generator in a barrow in the ground. It was not an ideal way of living. 'If we wanted to use the iron,' Juliet recalls ruefully, 'we couldn't have any lights on.' Their one 'luxury' was to attach a lorry battery to the television for Juliet's mother.

With the electricity sorted out, the couple's

Glass doors lead into the Gothic-inspired extension to the Arts and Crafts farmhouse. Architectural examples from this period can be seen throughout the house, such as the stained-glass windows emblazoned with the Bishop of London's crest. The guestroom has an old-fashioned Roberts radio and binoculars for bird-watching in the garden.

An Arts and Crafts doorway leads into the new custom-built kitchen, which features Gothic arches on the cupboards, shelving and windows to complement the design of the rest of the house. A sign-writer painted farmyard animals onto the cupboards, a visual reference to the organic farm outside.

PETER ATTRIBUTES HIS LOVE OF GOTHIC CATHEDRALS TO THE MANY HOURS HE SPENT AS A CHILD TRAWLING ROUND CHURCHES WITH HIS STONEMASON FATHER.

greatest extravagance – and most satisfying decision – was to lay wide boards of English oak for the kitchen floor, complementing the room's original Arts and Crafts chairs. Peter's brother cut the lettering for the drawers and cabinets, and a sign-writer provided the decorative designs for the cupboards. Taking their lead from the farmhouse's Arts and Crafts origins, Peter and Juliet installed copies of original doors and used William Morris prints for the sofas, cushions and curtains. Other furniture throughout the house was designed by the couple themselves, including the dining-room table, which was made by 'an alcoholic carpenter we had living in the barn'.

The parquet floor in the living room was rescued from a nunnery in Kennington, close to Peter and Juliet's south London home. Peter saw the flooring being dismantled, and managed to rescue it before it was sold off.

Installing the floor turned out to be a real labour of love as the parquet was embedded in mastic and every single block of wood had to be stripped by hand. The entire family chipped in, using only hot water to warm the wood and a scraper to prise the tar off with.

Favourite finds and belongings are found in the living room. On the near wall is a cast-iron stove, which one of Peter's authors at Dorling Kindersley discovered while writing a book on decorating. She convinced Peter to buy it and have it shipped from America. Juliet believes the stove to have Eastern European origins because of its similarity to a samovar. 'It must have been a real status symbol in North America,' she says, 'with so many immigrants from Eastern Europe bringing over these Russian-style stoves.'

Gathered around the fireplace are sofas and chairs from junk shops and auctions,

249

From the top-floor bedroom, an arched doorway opens out onto the cathedral-like space of the living room. William Morris prints have been used throughout the house on sofas, cushions and curtains.

which Juliet picked up in the 1980s. She admits to becoming 'totally obsessed with going to a particular auction once a month, in a barn down the road. I remember buying these two sofas for about £11 each.' The fireplace is from one of the smaller rooms in the basement at Castle Drogo, in Drewsteignton, which Juliet finds extraordinary considering the piece's size. 'Look how big it is!' she exclaims. 'And that was one of the tiniest fireplaces there.'

On the floor of the conservatory is one of the famous 'River' rugs designed by C. F. A. Voysey for Liberty. Juliet discovered the rug in the Liberty archive and commissioned one for the house, which was made by hand on a loom in India. Along the windowsill is a collection of battered straw hats, all of which have a history, to wear outside in the garden or while taking long walks on hot summer days.

One of Juliet's passions at Sheepdrove Farm is the flower-filled garden, which started out

as a formal design by John Brookes and is now all about colour and form. It is an organic garden, with a mix of flowers and vegetables to attract bees and butterflies. The incredibly realistic sculptures of Shetland sheep lend a playful element. Modelled on the terminal sires of the Kindersley flock and made from chicken wire, wool, straw, peat and fibre glass, the family bought the sheep from an art exhibition at the Soil Association's annual conference.

Peter and Juliet have worked as environmental campaigners for over thirty years, and today Sheepdrove Farm covers 2,250 acres and employs forty people. It is testament to their hard work and vision that they have been able to both build the house of their dreams and to create a farm that is truly sustainable, supporting wildlife and the environment.

A natural water filtration system is key to the organic farm. Plants and flowers that attract birds and insects frame the view to the nineteenth-century farmhouse. 'Children adore this house', Juliet says. 'Both Peter and I feel that houses should have some magic to them.'

IN KEEPING WITH THE ENVIRONMENTAL CONSCIOUSNESS OF SHEEPDROVE FARM, THE GARDEN'S BEAUTIFUL FLOWERS HAVE BEEN CHOSEN FOR THE LOCAL WILDLIFE.

FARMHOUSE ORGANIC

Devon Pottery

CLIVE BOWEN IS ONE OF ENGLAND'S leading potters and was the founder of Shebbear Pottery in Devon over thirty years ago. The wild landscape is of particular importance to his work, as is the use of 'simple local materials found within a few miles of my workshop'. Clive's farmhouse was also constructed from local materials, including bricks from the nearby clay pits. 'One of the reasons for settling in this remote part of north Devon', Clive explains, 'was the proximity to the clay pits at Fremington and Peters Marlow, and the abundance of sawmills providing waste wood for the kiln.'

Clive was working for a potter based in Barnstaple, in north Devon, when he and Rosie were married, and is still there today. The couple bought their farm and outbuildings from a local farmer, who had a smallholding with chickens and six cows. The sheds are now used for Shebbear Pottery's wood-fired kilns, while timber for the kiln and hay for the horses are stored on the other side of the barn.

One kiln holds 900 to 1,000 pots and is fired six times a year. The flames help to create both beautiful pots and some less beautiful ones, and Clive thrives on this element of chance. He is currently experimenting with porcelain, although he admits that 'this sort of porcelain was perfected centuries ago in China, and I'm just a studio potter struggling and trying to get it right'.

Leading into the house is a studio area for displaying Clive's pots and sculptures of horses by his daughter, Helena. The showroom was originally a wheelwright's shop and still has the old windows characteristic of this part of the country, comprised of whatever small, broken pieces of glass were to hand. Rosie explains that this was a kind of 'making do, and using odd bits of glass to create a patchwork effect in the windows'.

Rosie has a particular eye for colour and chose the vivid apple-green shade for the pantry, the deep cream for the kitchen, and the pale blue for the hallway. The same shade of blue was used for the front door. The kitchen is still an authentic Devon farmer's kitchen; the table was here when Clive and Rosie moved in, and the floor is laid with hand-made wire-cut bricks that were fired locally in Peters Marlow, a mere four miles away.

Around the Rayburn cooker, Rosie has arranged Clive's hand-made tiles, which with their rich green and earth-brown tones are perfectly in keeping with the natural feel of the place. Above the Rayburn is a collection of jugs that Clive started in the 1970s and 'intended to keep going, but which came to a stop'. Of particular importance is a nineteenth-century Devon jug. 'If you look at the shape,' Clive remarks, 'you will see the inspiration behind a lot of my work.'

Next to the Rayburn is a built-in settle made by Robinson Beach and intended for Clive's retirement. Because of its location in the warmest place in the house, the dogs have decided that it will suit them very well in the meantime. An ancient wooden rocking chair

'MY WAY OF WORKING IS A CONTINUATION OF GENERATIONS OF TRADITIONAL COUNTY POTTERS, WHOSE WORK HAS PROVIDED THE INSPIRATION FOR EVERYTHING I MAKE.'

that belonged to Rosie's father sits opposite the settle and alongside is a shelf, made from local wood and groaning under the weight of Rosie's cookery books. The shelf also acts as a division between the sitting room and kitchen, and was designed to keep the dogs out of the living area when necessary.

Looking into the sitting room, you see a beautiful cast-iron wood-burning stove that was given to Clive by a fellow potter in

DEVON POTTERY

White duck eggs are collected in a wicker basket and Clive's pots are arranged in front of the studio window, made in the traditional local method of using different sized panes of glass. The horse sculptures are by Clive and Rosie's daughter, Helena, who trained as a zoologist at Bristol University.

recognition of Clive's fascination with the wood-burning process. This Ulefos stove dates to 1914, and was originally made for a railway station in Norway. The elegant wooden parquet floor in this room was put down by Commander King of the British Navy, one of the former owners of the farm. Across the hallway is the music room, with a nineteenth-century Beulhoff piano and a library of books collected by the couple over the last twenty years.

CLIVE WORKS WITH A VERY SMALL RANGE OF MATERIALS, JUST EARTHENWARE CLAY AND COLOURED SLIPS (LIQUID CLAYS), ONE OF WHICH COMES FROM HIS FIELD.

Clive makes a point of creating pieces that are functional as well as beautiful, and makes coffee cups, mugs and fruit bowls to use in the kitchen. Logs are stacked in the living room next to the cast-iron Ulefos stove from Norway.

The pots in the sitting room and kitchen were made by fellow potters, and even by some visiting Japanese artists. 'As you can see,' Clive observes, 'the shelves are a bit crowded, but there are pieces that go back a long way and were made by many different friends.'

Clive is very keen that everything that he makes is useful, rather than merely beautiful: 'I enjoy sitting at the table eating with friends, and my preoccupation is always with the function of the pieces. I want my pots to be used, not merely to sit in isolation on a shelf.'

CLIVE DESCRIBES HIS COLLECTION OF JUGS
AS 'VERY GOOD FRIENDS AND NEIGHBOURS
COLLECTED OVER THE YEARS'.

Contemporary Country

COWLEY MANOR, CHELTENHAM, GLOUCESTERSHIRE

WHEN TRAVELLING AROUND ENGLAND, Jessica and Peter Sainsbury found most country hotels to be 'too stuffy or old-fashioned', and admit that there was nowhere that they really liked to stay. Inspired to create their own relaxed country-house hotel, the couple began the search for a suitable property. Six months later, Jessica and Peter discovered Cowley Manor and realized the moment they saw it that it was 'the grounds that set Cowley apart and made it truly exceptional'.

After years of institutional use, Cowley Manor was in a pretty sorry state when the couple purchased it. Most of the rooms had been subdivided, and there was no longer any sense of their former proportions. Jessica knocked down walls and returned the rooms to the scale of a private home; where there were once thirty bedrooms in the main house, there are now only fifteen luxuriously-spaced suites.

The design of the house was a collaborative effort between the Sainsburys and architectural firm De Matos Storey Ryan, together with furniture-makers Kay+Stemmer and textile designers Mei-Ha Tsang and Govindia Hemphill, and followed Jessica's brief that the hotel be 'modern, but not minimal'. Green is the signature Cowley Manor colour, and there are three different shades used for the textiles, furniture and walls throughout the house. Aiming for 'tasteful clashing', the design team used liberal splashes of warm colour; as a result, nothing in the house matches, but neither are there any jarring colours. Jessica chose to paint only one wall in a bright colour, rather than the entire room, 'which would have been too overwhelming'.

To decorate the house, the couple sought out work by young artists at degree shows and auctions. The very first pieces of contemporary art that Jessica bought were the papier-mâché animal heads, which she thought were 'an amusing take on traditional hunting trophies', and they now have pride of place in the bar. She admits that after a particularly overindulgent evening, one

The colour green is everywhere at Cowley, and can be seen in the upholstered oak dining chairs and the uplit ceiling in the bar. Original detailing in the dining room includes the oak panelling and parquet floor, which date back to 1895.

'WHEN I WALKED AROUND THE LAKE AND CAME ACROSS CASCADES OF FOUNTAINS, I KNEW THAT THE GROUNDS MADE COWLEY MANOR TRULY EXCEPTIONAL.'

alarmed guest thought that they were real.

Architects from De Matos Storey Ryan explain that 'once the spaces of the original house had been re-established, strong colour and tactile natural materials were used to define the character of each room'. The bedroom furniture was designed by Kay+Stemmer, including the streamlined four-poster beds made of oak, wardrobes, desks, chairs and coffee tables, and templates were

The apple-green sitting room leads through to the chic modern bar, with its chocolate-brown walls and leather seating. The bookend seats were designed by Italian design firm Ceccotti, and the sofas are from Coexistence, in London.

shown to the entire design team. The architects designed the oak seating and shelving in collaboration with Mei-Ha Tsang, who also made the cushions and curtains.

There are fifteen stable block rooms, consisting of two-storey and three-storey suites, which were designed to be open-plan, loft-style areas. The larger suites have a ground-floor sitting room, a bathroom on the first floor, and a top-floor bedroom, whereas the smaller suites have a ground-floor bedroom and living area, with a bathroom suspended on the floor above. Jessica feels that these are the most exciting rooms in the hotel in terms of design, but as they are quite narrow, they do not have quite the same feeling of space as in the main house.

'It is one of the luxuries of modern life to lounge in the bath', Jessica declares, and she has decreed that the bathrooms should be the last word in ultimate extravagance. At Cowley, each bathroom is the size of an average London bedroom, complete with huge windows and a freestanding bath and shower. Jessica wanted a double-ended bath in each room, and, when looking for fixtures and fittings, she climbed into showroom baths to test the proportions despite being heavily pregnant. She recommends Room 17 because the bathtub can 'fit two people in it'.

There are no antiques at Cowley Manor, which is furnished with bespoke pieces by Kay+Stemmer. Jessica specified oak furniture for all of the rooms, reflecting the Cotswolds Arts and Crafts movement. The tables and chairs in the restaurant are custom-made and upholstered in Cowley green.

When Cowley Manor was designed in the

late nineteenth century, it was a fairly luxurious stately home and even had a Turkish bath in the main house. To bring Cowley into the twenty-first century, Jessica was keen to design a state-of-the-art spa alongside the house. The result is the wittily named 'C-Side' spa, complete with treatments exclusive to Cowley, including aromatherapy by Michelle Roques-O'Neill, who embraces such new-age concepts as chakra lines to de-stress her clients. The spa also has an indoor swimming pool, which was designed to be particularly long and wide, thus ensuring that it never feels too crowded.

Architect Angus Morrogh-Ryan envisioned the pool as 'an enclosed landscape, with a planted roof of lavender'. Completely enclosed by huge glass panels, the pool has views across the surrounding countryside. The dry-stone wall leading up to the spa was taken from the local vernacular, the opposite wall is made from dressed, cast stone, echoing the smooth stone walls of the house, and the third wall is lined with grey-green Welsh slate. The slate was repeated on the floor of the pool, with the wet and dry tiles creating beautifully contrasting colours. The outdoor pool is heated all year round, allowing adventurous guests to have a dip in January.

Life at Cowley is lived at a leisurely, relaxed pace, from having long, pampering soaks in the bath, to putting your feet up on the table and reading your way through the weekend papers. This country hotel offers the ultimate in laid-back luxury.

The oak-panelled bathroom has a freestanding bath by Kaldewei, with taps and fittings by Dornbracht. Bespoke designs from Mei-Ha Tsang are visible in the unique throws and cushions in the bedroom. Round chairs by Coexistence are placed in the stylish spa area, overlooking the indoor pool made from Welsh slate.

COWLEY MANOR'S MODERN TAKE ON COUNTRY RUSTICITY REPLACES CHINTZY CLUTTER WITH WARMTH AND LUXURY.

Directory

ARCHITECTS, ARTISTS AND DESIGNERS

Petra Boase [200]
Textile Designer
Tel/Fax: 01366 328 232
www.petraboase.com

Clive Bowen [254]
Ceramicist
Shebbear Pottery
Shebbear, Beaworthy, Devon EX21 5QZ
Tel: 01409 281 271
Email: bowenpottery@compuserve.com

Shaun Clarkson [122]
Interior Designer
Shaun Clarkson ID
Tel: 020 7739 6865
Fax: 020 7739 6864
Email: mail@shaunclarkson.com
www.shaunclarkson.com

Chris Cowper [178]
Architect
Cowper Griffith Architects
15 High Street, Whittlesford,
Cambridge CB2 4LT
Tel: 01223 835 998
Fax: 01223 837 327
Email: architects@cowpergriffith.co.uk
www.cowpergriffith.co.uk

Henrietta Faire [208]
Fashion Designer
Stokers, Gong Lane, Burnham Overy Staithe,
Kings Lynn, Norfolk PE31 8JG
Tel: 01328 730 740
Email: henriettafaire@yahoo.co.uk

Thomas Faire [208]
Architect
Ulph Place, Burnham Market, Kings Lynn,
Norfolk PE31 8EL
Tel/Fax: 01328 738 276

Kaffe Fassett [216]
Textile Designer
Kaffe Fassett Studio
www.kaffefassett.com

Cassian Garbett [160]
Woodcarver and Furniture-Maker
Email: info@cassianfurniture.co.uk
www.cassianfurniture.co.uk

Patrick Lynch [68]
Architect
Lynch Architects
147A Hoxton Street, London N1 6QG
Tel: 020 7739 5760
Email: lyncharchitects@btopenworld.com
www.lyncharchitects.co.uk

Brandon Mably [216]
Textile Designer
Brandon Mably Designs
Email: brandon@brandonmably.com
www.brandonmably.com

Peter Marlow [168]
Photographer
Magnum Photos
5 Old Street, London EC1V 9HL
Tel: 020 7490 1771
Fax: 020 7608 0020
Email: websitemail@petermarlow.com
www.petermarlow.com

David Murray [236]
Furniture-Maker
Email: david@quercusbluff.freeserve.co.uk

Fiona Naylor [168]
Architect
Johnson Naylor
13 Britton Street, London EC1M 5SX
Tel: 020 7490 8885
Fax: 020 7490 0038
Email: jn@johnsonnaylor.co.uk
www.johnsonnaylor.co.uk

Richard Parr [28]
Architect
Parrwalker & Associates Ltd
Easter Park, Nymphsfield,
Gloucestershire GL10 3UL
Tel: 01453 860 200
Fax: 01453 861 699
Email: info@parrwalker.com
www.parrwalker.com

Diana and Simon Sieff [58]
Interior Designers
Sieff Ltd
49 Long Street, Tetbury,
Gloucestershire GL8 8AA
Tel: 01666 504 477
Fax: 01666 504 478
Email: sieff@sieff.co.uk
www.sieff.co.uk

HOTELS

Babington House [132]
Babington, Frome, Somerset BA11 3RW
Tel: 01373 812 266
Fax: 01373 812 112
Email: enquiries@babingtonhouse.co.uk
www.babingtonhouse.co.uk

Cowley Manor [262]
Cowley, Cheltenham, Gloucestershire GL53 9NL
Tel: 01242 870 900
Fax: 01242 870 901
Email: stay@cowleymanor.com
www.cowleymanor.com

Fowey Hall [224]
Hanson Drive, Fowey, Cornwall PL23 1ET
Tel: 01726 833 866
Fax: 01726 834 100
Email: info@foweyhall.com
www.luxuryfamilyhotels.com

Hotel Tresanton [186]
St Mawes, Cornwall TR2 5DR
Tel: 01326 270 055
Fax: 01326 270 053
Email: info@tresanton.com
www.tresanton.com

The Ickworth Hotel [78]
Horringer, Bury St Edmunds, Suffolk IP29 5QE
Tel: 01284 735 350
Fax: 01284 736 300
Email: info@ickworthhotel.com
www.luxuryfamilyhotels.com

The Victoria Hotel [38]
Park Road, Holkham, Wells-Next-the-Sea,
Norfolk NR23 1RG
Tel: 01328 711 008
www.holkham.co.uk/victoria

PLACES TO VISIT

Hartland Abbey [112]
Hartland, Bideford, Devon EX39 6DT
Tel: 01237 441 234
Fax: 01237 441 264
Email: ha_admin@btconnect.com
www.hartlandabbey.com

Clovelly Village [146]
Visitor Centre
Clovelly, Bideford, Devon EX39 5TA
Tel: 01237 431 781
Email: cec@clovelly.co.uk
www.clovelly.co.uk

PROPERTIES TO RENT

Cliff Barns [122]
Foulden, Thetford, Norfolk IP26 5WS
Tel: 01366 328 342
Fax: 01366 328 942
Email: info@cliffbarns.com
www.cliffbarns.com

Island House [178]
Chris Cowper
Email: chris@cowpergriffith.co.uk

FARM

Sheepdrove Organic Farm [244]
Lambourn, Berkshire RG17 7UU
Tel: 01488 674 700
Tel (shop): 01488 71659
Fax: 01488 72677
www.sheepdrove.com